The Revd Prebendary Desmond Tillyer is the author of two books on contemplative prayer, based on the teaching of St John of the Cross. After his title parish, he worked as chaplain of Liddon House at the Grosvenor Chapel in Mayfair, caring for new university graduates and newly qualified teachers, recommended forward by university and college of education chaplains. This was followed by 32 years as Vicar of St Peter's Eaton Square until retirement in 2006.

For Ron, Richard, Christopher and Jeffrey

Desmond Tillyer

WATERS OF LOVE

Ivy Goodley and Martin Israel

AUSTIN MACAULEY PUBLISHERS™

LONDON * CAMBRIDGE * NEW YORK * SHARJAH

A CIP catalogue record for this title is available from the British Library.

ISBN 9781398451148 (Paperback)
ISBN 9781398451155 (ePub e-book)

www.austinmacauley.com

First Published 2023
Austin Macauley Publishers Ltd®
1 Canada Square
Canary Wharf
London
E14 5AA

My hope and purpose in publishing this book is to fulfil Ivy Goodley's intention that, as her literary executor, I should make her life's work more widely known and be of benefit to others. She herself was highly sceptical of this project and only Martin Israel's persistence won her over to the task.

My thanks to Ivy's family for their patience as I set out on this task, to Jeff Goodley for his permission to publish the photograph of his mother in Holbeach, The Revd Alan Chidwick for helping with the proofreading, to The Revd Dr Philip Krinks's help in finding a publisher and to Hymns Ancient and Modern for permission to include the sermon preached by Austin Farrer for *All Souls' Day*.

Foreword

This book has a twofold purpose. First, it is to fulfil the wishes of Ivy Goodley that her Christian experiences be published after her death. However, while reading her writings, a second reason emerged when it became clear, reading through her Spiritual Diary, her autobiography and the letters in her archive, that a remarkable relationship with The Revd. Dr Martin Israel developed between them from 1976 right up to Martin's death in 2007.

Therefore, the book is shaped by these two mutually developing themes of "visionary" experience and growing interdependence between two remarkable people brought together by their common commitment to Christ and his Gospel.

However, before we can proceed to consider these two remarkable people, one a well-known and highly influential priest, retreat conductor, confessor and spiritual director, exorcist and deliverance minister, the other an unknown housewife, married to a plumber, mother of three sons, living in Walthamstow in East London, worshipping at an ordinary parish church, dedicated to St Michael and All Angels and later, after the death of her husband, living in the market town of Holbeach in Lincolnshire, more needs to be said about the background to their experience and the way it which it is presented in this book.

Both Ivy and Martin founded their lives and ministries on the practice of prayer. This fundamental, traditional emphasis is there in the New Testament and in the witness of the early Church. Furthermore, from those beginnings, there quickly emerged a universal acceptance that because God is by definition incomprehensible, that is to say, beyond our intellectual capacity to define, our emotional power to grasp and our intuitive sense to penetrate, the practice of prayer for every Christian should, if persisted through various times of change and loss of the familiar, develop from mental prayer and meditation, involving the making of images of God and using our intellectual, emotional, imaginative and intuitive powers to deepen our understanding of our faith and discipleship, into something very different. This different thing is called contemplation, which is simply living a life of prayer beyond words, ideas, images, entering into the hidden presence of God where there are no words, no ideas, no images, but only darkness in which the absence of God is also his presence and the darkness is, in fact, the means of approaching the unapproachable light of God. We see in the history of the Church in every age those who speak in these terms. The list of names is inexhaustible, but examples would include Irenaeus, the Cappadocian Fathers, Gregory the Great, Augustine of Hippo, Benedict, Dionysius the Areopagite, Anselm, Francis and Dominic, Gregory Palamas, Hildegard of Bingen, Thomas Aquinas, Catherine of Sienna. Catherine of Genoa, Mother Julian of Norwich, Richard Rolle, the unknown author of *The Cloud of Unknowing*, Walter Hilton, Meister Eckhart, etc.

Two of the greatest exponents of this tradition in the twentieth century were Austin Farrer in the period after the Second World War and Bishop Kenneth Kirk, Bishop of Oxford, whose Bampton Lectures of 1928 *called The Vision of God* expounded this tradition right through the history of the Church until the Reformation, when in a section called *The Reversal of Tradition*, he expounds how the consequences of the Reformation led to the loss of this universal understanding of the role of prayer to lead us all to contemplation into an attempt to regulate it as either an aberration or something to be tightly controlled. Both Reformation and Counter-Reformation movements feared the loss of control by authority over the lives of their members. Reformers reacted by declaring contemplation an unacceptable way of prayer because it potentially undermines the control of those in authority. The Council of Trent could not deny the tradition but sought to restrict the practice of contemplation to 'professional' Christians, that is, the ordained and monks, nuns and friars, with everyone else restricted to mental prayer and meditation. Of course, there were those who resisted these restrictions. Outstanding examples are Teresa of Avila, John of the Cross, Pere Grou, de Caussade. Baron Von Hugel, among others, including in England Evelyn Underhill, Dean Harton and Dom John Chapman. It was into this tradition that Ivy and Martin enter a shop each experienced the call to prayer and took it seriously.

But if contemplation is seen in the tradition from the start as the goal for all Christians, other spiritual gifts such as the call to be a visionary are much rarer. Indeed, the use of the word 'visionary' is itself misleading, since the witness of all visionaries is that nothing is actually seen. Rather, they use the language of the five senses, sight, hearing, touch, taste and smell as analogous to their experience. They use it because what they transmit to them is beyond words, beyond the intellect, beyond the imagination, beyond the emotions, beyond the intuition, beyond the senses. Only when what is perceived is written down, does language have to be found to describe inadequately what is experienced. What is communicated by words is but a form of communication that is necessary but not sufficient. This is where the use of the language of the five senses and the imagination begins to be used. It was into this particular grace that Ivy found herself entering in 1976, and she was totally unprepared for it. Her Spiritual Diary begins about this time and we read of a rapid development in which she struggles to find a framework within which even to begin to articulate what is happening, both within herself and her own self-understanding and to her Spiritual Diary as the 'visions' begin to unfold.

Each visionary has a particular way of experiencing these visionary moments. For example, in the case of Mother Julian of Norwich, hers occurred over a short time after she recovered from a nearly fatal illness. Ivy, in contrast, has visionary experiences which develop slowly and usually emerge gradually over several weeks or months. This means that there is much repetition and many unexpected developments that add to the richness of the experience. This also means that it is impossible within the compass of this book to include all her experience, but a selection has to be made that will represent the range of experience that she underwent.

Also, because Ivy wrote down everything she experienced, her writings are usually quite long. Because her education was not adequate and her innate intelligence did not emerge until secondary education, and even then was not properly nurtured, Ivy's way of writing does need some explanation. First, she rarely writes in discrete sentences, but rather a flow of clauses linked with commas. Generally speaking, I have left her style as it is, in order to reveal her authentic voice, but sometimes, when the sentences become too complex, it has been necessary to break them down into two or three sentences to make them comprehensible. Secondly, I have corrected some spelling. Just occasionally, because her handwriting is quite difficult to read, if I cannot work out a word or phrase I leave a gap. If there is a need for an explanation, I put one in briefly in italics, taking care not to change the sense of what is there. At times, to protect the identity of individuals, Ivy may use the letter X or, more often, one or more of the initials of the name of the person concerned. I have left these in place unless the person can be identified from the context and/or the initial and is still alive.

Finally, there is the issue of the validity of these experiences. Ivy's faith, moulded and developed in an Anglo-Catholic parish, is clearly rooted in that tradition, expressed by the Catholic Creeds, the Church's liturgical year, the practice of regular sacramental life. However, there are occasionally particular expressions of faith, in particular, the conviction that the life beyond death is a learning experience illuminated by the ultimate victory of Christ's Resurrection over sin and death, so that although the transition may be painful and hard, nevertheless, Hell does not have the last word for anyone. (This universalism is in fact a common conviction of the vast majority of those whose prayer is contemplative.) Also, her visionary experience of the progress of the human soul to Heaven is thoroughly orthodox. The incomprehensible nature of God means that we proceed in this life by grace towards the vision of God but it also means that life beyond death is also led by grace, so that the vision of God is not being led into his essence but by his grace into the fulfilling glory of his presence. The boundary between the uncreated and the created, the infinite and the finite, the eternal and the temporal remains, but that which is created is fulfilled. As St Augustine puts it, 'We shall see and we shall know, we shall know and we shall love, we shall love and we shall praise, in the end that has no end.' In Ivy's visions of the progress of the soul into a relationship with eternity, as it reaches the final step towards the vision of God, Ivy's experience withdraws from the boundary, knowing that beyond is the incomprehensible God.

Therefore, this book divides into three sections. First a short biography of Ivy Goodley. Secondly, the consideration of the relationship between Ivy and Martin Israel, revealed through the references to him in her Spiritual Diary and his 45 letters to her that remain in her archive. Thirdly, the introductory visions from 1976 onwards, followed a series of mature visions focused on different aspects of her experience. Finally, a selection of her last entries in the Spiritual Diary while living in Holbeach.

In the first decade of the twenty-first century, a newly ordained priest in East Anglia asked me if I could recommend a spiritual director to him not too far away from his title parish. I recommended Ivy to him. 'Ah,' he replied. 'I have heard a rumour of a holy woman at Holbeach.' That woman was Ivy Goodley.

Chapter 1
An Introduction to the Life of
Ivy Margaret Goodley (1918–2012)

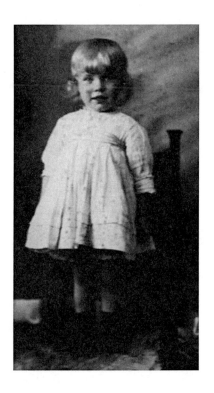

Ivy, aged 7, standing on a chair, just days before she was put into workhouse.

This book is about the life and spiritual experiences of Ivy Margaret Goodley and her relationship with the Revd Dr Martin Israel. It was my privilege to know her as a friend from 1962 until her death in 2012. Her life was rooted in the mystical tradition of the Christian Church and in her experience of hardness, sorrow and joy in Walthamstow in East London. However, in order to understand the mystical tradition that she imbibed and was eventually the foundation of her whole life, it will help us to begin in a very different setting.

Shortly after the ending of the Second World War, a preacher delivered a sermon in All Souls' College, Oxford. He was Austin Farrer, one of the most brilliant minds to have articulated the Christian faith in England in the twentieth century. What he preached was this:

"'May they rest in peace and may light perpetual shine upon them'—those millions among whom our friends are lost, those millions for whom we cannot choose but pray; because prayer is a sharing in the love in the heart of God, and the love of God is earnestly set towards the salvation of his spiritual creatures, by, through and out of the fire that purifies them."

"The arithmetic of death perplexes our brains. What can we do but throw ourselves upon the infinity of God? It is only to a finite mind that number is an obstacle, or multiplicity a distraction. Our mind is like a box of limited content, out of which one thing must be emptied before another can find a place. The universe of creatures is queuing for a turn of our attention and no appreciable part of the queue will ever get a turn. But no queue forms before the throne of everlasting mercy, because the nature of an infinite mind is to be simply aware of all that is."

"Everything is simply present to an infinite mind because it exists; or rather, exists because it is present to that making mind. And though by some process of averaging and calculation, I should compute the grains of sand, it would be like the arithmetic of the departed souls, an empty sum; I could not tell them as they are told in the infinity of God's counsels, each one separately present as what it is, and simply because it is."

"The thought God gives to any of his creatures is not measured by the attention he can spare, but by the object for consideration they can supply. God is not divided; it is God, not a part of God, who applies himself to the falling sparrow, and to the crucified Lord. But there is more in the beloved Son than in the sparrow, to be observed and loved and saved by God. So every soul that has passed out of this visible world, as well as every soul remaining within it, is caught and held in the unwavering beam of divine care. And we may comfort ourselves for our own inability to tell the grains of sand or to reckon the thousands of millions of the departed."

"And yet, we cannot altogether escape so; for our religion is not a simple relation of every soul separately to God, it is a mystical body in which we are all members one of another. And in this mystical body, it does not suffice that every soul should be embraced by the thoughts of God; it is also to be that every soul should, in its thought, embrace the other souls. For apart from this mutual embracing, it would be unintelligible why we should pray at all, either for the living or for the departed. Such prayer is nothing but the exercising of our membership in the body of Christ. God is not content to care for us each severally, unless he can also, by his Holy Spirit in each one of us, care through and in us for all the rest. Every one of us is to be a focus of that divine life of which the attractive power holds the body together in one."

"So even in the darkness and blindness of our present existence, our thought ranges abroad and spreads out towards the confines of the mystical Christ, remembering the whole Church of Christ, as well militant on earth as triumphant in heaven; invoking angels, archangels and all the spiritual hosts."

This sermon, preached in Oxford, sets out in highly wrought, intellectual terms the vision of God as the infinite Love which creates, knows, saves and brings us all together into a fulfilment which is nothing less than eternal life, experienced through faith by grace now and hereafter by grace, seeing him as he is. (1 John 3)

It is pretty certain that Ivy Goodley never read this sermon or even that she knew who Austin Farrer was. However, what Austin Farrer is describing and what Ivy experienced in her life of prayer and mystical experience is the same thing, expressed in different terms but carrying the same meaning, namely, the corporate nature of our relationship with God, bound together in one life, the risen life of Christ, both here and in our destiny in eternity, that Love is the nature of God, that love is the nature of human life as God intended it, and that in the end "nothing can separate us from the love of God in Christ Jesus" (Romans 8), despite the reality of sin and human suffering as two of the constants in human experience.

A more direct source of inspiration for Ivy came from Julian of Norwich and her book "Revelations of Divine Love" though she did not read the entire book until 1982, long after she began her spiritual journey in earnest in 1976. From Julian came, via T.S. Elliot, the words, "All shall be well and all manner of things shall be well." These words became for her a motif by which she interpreted the ultimate triumph of the love of God, of the God who is Love.

Then there is the third element in God's preparation of Ivy for her vocation. In 1974, she visited the Anglican Benedictine Abbey of West Mailing, in Kent, where she developed a spiritual relationship with the Guest Sister, Anastasia. While there standing beside the stream that flows through the abbey grounds, the words came to her "Lead gently by the still waters of love." This, together with Julian's saying, became the recurring theme of her mystical experience. Hence the title of this book.

However, Ivy started life in very different circumstances. She was born at 52, Buxton Road, Walthamstow, Essex (now London E. 17) on 11 April 1917. Her mother was Mahaliah Pickett, a tram conductress, daughter of Jack Pickett, together with Nancy and four other children. Her step grandmother's name is unknown, she never mentions it, a stern and hard woman, who disliked her. Ivy never knew her father. She was illegitimate, and all she knew was that he was a local policeman, but never discovered more. Her mother's name comes from a very obscure, minor figure in the Old Testament and is very unusual. Why was she called this? It is a mystery, compared with the ordinary names of her siblings. Interestingly, many years later, when Ivy was living in Holbeach, Lincolnshire, she wrote this on 26 October 1994. "A list was posted this morning at the back of church for those we remember on All Souls Day. I put my mother's name, and it wasn't until halfway through the service that I realised I had written "May Pickett," her maiden name instead of her married name "Hills, Why on earth did I do this? What was in my mind?" Interestingly, Ivy refers only to the surname, not also to her mother's Christian name, which is also wrong. There is a mystery here.

Mahaliah, did not want the child and tried to abort it, but was unsuccessful. Ivy weighed only three pounds at birth and was not really expected to survive, but she did. Her mother did not want her, her step grandmother showed no love towards her. The family shame was such that she was not baptised in the parish church, St Michael and all Angels, Walthamstow, but in the next-door Parish of St Saviour's, where Nancy and a friend of hers, Margaret King, were the godmothers. Hence, her second name is Margaret, though why she was called Ivy is unknown. Both these women wanted to become nuns but neither was successful because they could not conform to the vow of obedience required of them and both, after attempts at several communities, failed to enter the religious life and became embittered. Nancy, however, did play a key role in Ivy's life, and without her, it would have been even more difficult than it became. Ivy says in her autobiography that the only person who loved her was her grandfather.

When she was 19 months old, her mother married a man called William Hills, a drunkard. They lived in two rooms in her grandparents' house, Ivy sleeping in a chair bedstead behind the kitchen door, with a knitted patchwork quilt that Ivy could picture even in her adulthood. When she heard the steps of her stepfather on the stairs, she soon learned to pull the quilt up over her head. In 1924, William and Mahaliah had a daughter called Kathleen. When she was born, he disappeared and was never seen again.

Mother and daughters continued to live in the family house. Later, mother joined the Salvation Army causing upset in the home, but here Ivy got her first experience of Christian worship and enjoyed it. She went to the local primary school in Pretoria Avenue. She remembered herself as not an easy child, but strong-willed and rebellious. As she grew, she became a tomboy, preferring to play with the boys and getting up to all sorts of mischief. However, in 1925, when she was seven, the whole of her life changed. Her mother suffered from tuberculosis on and off for a long time. At the age of seven and Kathleen aged one, their mother had to go away for treatment. The family situation must have been bad because she would not leave either of them there while she was away. Instead, they took a tram for what seemed a long journey, in fact, to just outside Leytonstone, the next-door suburb, to a place called later Langthorne House, then called simply The Workhouse. The memory of that day remained etched into Ivy's memory – the tram ride, the long walk up the drive, the massive gates at the entrance, the fact that they were evidently expected. A nurse was waiting for them. Her mother handed Kathleen to her and pushed Ivy forward. She did not speak, did not say 'goodbye', but turned and walked through the iron gates and was gone. She did not see Kathleen again for a very long time and had no idea what happened to her. Ivy was led into a room full of old people – all women – sitting motionless at a long table, their faces devoid of expression and silent, into another small room where she was undressed and washed with carbolic soap. Her hair was cut short. In the evening, she was put to sleep in an iron bed.

After a period of time, Ivy was transferred to an orphanage at Wanstead and from there to what was known as a 'cottage home' at Woodford. These would now be called 'foster homes'. When she was about eight years old, Ivy developed a severe attack of measles and was taken to Whipps Cross Hospital in Leytonstone, where one day she saw her mother and another woman walk by. She found herself unable to call out to her so that she passed by without being aware of her. She never saw her mother again but learned in 1927 that she had died of bowel cancer, aged 32. After this, Ivy was returned to her grandparents and Kathleen returned to her father's parents. They both lived in Walthamstow and met occasionally. When Ivy was 23 years old and Kathleen was 17 years old, she came to say goodbye, saying she was going to join the Army. She never heard from her again and many years later tried to find her but was unsuccessful.

In the meantime, her grandparents died, each of cancer, after a life of grinding poverty, their daughter and her aunt, Nancy, took Ivy in to give her a home. The tomboy girl made life difficult for her unmarried aunt, money was always tight, her main friends were boys from whom she learned to climb trees over the wall into the cellars of the local brewery and smoke brown paper rolled up cigarette fashion. Nevertheless, Nancy brought Ivy up to go to church and she was confirmed and became a communicant member of St Paul's Courtenay Road, a daughter church of St Michael and all Angels' church. This St Paul's church was demolished in the mid-1960s.

Each August, Ivy would go to stay with another aunt and uncle in Manchester. Theirs was a childless marriage, an ectopic pregnancy early in the marriage, leading to a hysterectomy which nearly killed the aunt, resulting in the end of sexual relations between them. The uncle was said to be extremely fond of children and worked for various charities by singing at fundraising concerts. Having a young girl in the house proved too much temptation for him and he tried many times during her visits to have sexual intercourse with her, but he never succeeded. Ivy had no idea what he was trying to do, only that she was frightened and 'fought like a little cat' to stop him. It always happened when the aunt was out of the house. Sometimes the uncle would visit his sister, Nancy, with whom Ivy lived and tried the same assaults on her while Nancy was not present. Many years later, when he was dying, his wife, not realising what had happened in the past, asked Ivy, now married to Ron and a mother of children, to come to see him before he died. In order to go, Ivy had to cash in a small life insurance policy, taken out to cover funerary expenses so that she could afford the train fare and make the journey to Manchester. There, at the end of his life, he tried once more to seduce her. She just moved out of reach and left as soon as she decently could. He died soon after. Nancy knew nothing of her brother's behaviour and Ivy felt no harm had come to her because of her uncle's attempts to assault her, partly because of ignorance of the facts of life at the beginning and later because she knew what to expect and continued to repulse him. Her aunt in Manchester never knew.

Ivy left school before she was 15 years old, her primary education had been very basic. For example, all her life, her use of language was idiosyncratic. She strung sentences together, using commas, her spelling remained erratic and her handwriting difficult at times to decipher. On the other hand, her move to secondary school around the age of eleven did bring out her innate intelligence, so that she did well in all but one subject in examinations and came out first in her class. The exception was needlework, something which she never mastered. It did not interest her.

She wanted to work with animals but this was not allowed and was put as an apprentice hairdresser for three years, paid 2/6 per week for the first year, 5/- per week for the second year and 7/6 per week for the third year. (This amounts to twelve and a half pence, 25 pence and thirty-seven and a half pence respectively in current money.) She hated the work and eventually left to take up other shop work, including a time in Sainsbury's. Then came the Second World War and she was faced with the choice of joining the Land Army or becoming a motor mechanic.

By this time, she had met Ronald Goodley, her future husband, who had not yet been called up, and she chose to become a motor mechanic to stay near him. She had met Ron at a cycling club in July 1939. They courted for over three years, and Ivy called his courtship hilarious. She was a little older than he but they were both emotionally young. He was often nervous and unsure of himself, but they had a very happy courtship and her strong sense of Cockney humour developed. This and her raucous laugh remained with her throughout her life. Ron was giving her a sense of security and happiness, which was his great gift to their successful marriage. He was serving an apprenticeship as a plumber/sanitary engineer. They became engaged when he was called up in 1942 and subsequently went into the Air Force as a coppersmith/sheet metalworker. They were married on 24 January 1943, a white wedding in a borrowed dress at St Paul's Church, Courtenay Road, by a priest Ivy greatly admired, Father Ernest Bishop, whom she described as 'a truly lovely and understanding man'. Nancy tried to prevent the marriage, producing all sorts of excuses – There's a war on – You've no money – He's not good enough for you – while the real reason for her opposition was the secret knowledge that Ivy was illegitimate. Clearly, Nancy hoped that Ivy, like her, would never marry and, therefore, never discover the truth. Ivy was now 24 years old when she learned that she was illegitimate. She had always believed that her father had been killed in the First World War. She was deeply shocked but knew that she had to tell Ron. She was frightened he would reject her but his reply on being told was, 'I am marrying you, not what your mother or father have done.' They then told Fr Bishop who replied, 'You love each other, nothing else matters.' When they came to sign the marriage certificate after the marriage, Fr Bishop placed his hand in such a way that it completely covered where it said 'Father's name and profession'. She never forgot him and 30 years later, traced him to Prestatyn in North Wales and went to see him. She remembered the visit as a truly lovely meeting. Six months later, his daughter sent them a notice from a newspaper to say that he had died.

Shortly after the wedding, Ivy first developed appendicitis and quickly afterwards needed to have her gall bladder removed. Both of these operations were done at the Jewish Hospital in Whitechapel. Then in 1945, she became pregnant with her first child. The baby was a boy. Before the baby was born, Ivy and Ron had discussed names and, if it were a boy, chose the name, Richard John. He was stillborn, suffering from hydrocephalus. It was a long and dangerous delivery, ending up with surgery. The shock and pain of his loss, after carrying what was a living child in her womb, drove Ivy into such distress that she did not know what happened to the child's body and it was only years later that her third son, Jeffrey, found out that he had been buried in Chingford Cemetery. Besides the loss of the child. Ivy also lost all faith in God and for sixteen years did not return to church. She refused to discuss the child with her husband or Fr Bishop.

However, fairly soon afterwards, she conceived again and Christopher was born and thrived. Fr Bishop baptised him, he proved an easy child to bring up and some years later when Ivy realised that his name means 'Christ-bearer', this became a sign to her of his later vocation to become a priest, which he did. A third pregnancy followed four years later and Jeffrey was born. As a child, he went of his own volition to Sunday school and had a good voice in the church choir. When he grew up, he joined the police. As he said, "I guess it's in the genes!" The family was still living with Nancy which created tensions between the two women but eventually, when the boys were seven and two years of age, Ron managed to save enough money by working away from home to put down a deposit on their own house, which they moved into, 101, Salop Road, Walthamstow. Later, as a teenager, Christopher developed petit mal after an attack of scarlet fever but managed to pursue his schooling and eventually his vocation. Meanwhile, Nancy visited the family in their new home, twice a week and the tensions between aunt and niece remained as Nancy tried to interfere in the upbringing of the children and Ivy struggled with the memories of her upbringing by her aunt, while also being grateful that she took her in after her grandparents died. This tension was not resolved until just before Nancy died on 15 May 1980. Ron died on 3 May 1984, at the young age of 63 from heart attacks, probably brought on by his professional work with lead. He was buried in the Queen's Road Cemetery, Walthamstow. It was a sadness that remained with her, after the fulfilling experience of a very happy marriage, while at the same time she was upheld by her faith and mystical experience, which gave her an objective and a balance that sustained her until her final days. He had always given her the space to follow her own spiritual path and supported her, often without understanding where she went or what she was doing or who was coming for meetings and masses in the house. One particular example of his incomprehension and sense of humour, was when she asked him if he minded her putting a crucifix on a wall in the house. He replied, "Not at all. I'm not anti-Semitic."

How Ivy came back to faith is as follows. Sixteen years after Richard John had been stillborn, in June 1962, a new priest, Fr Michael Chaffey, was inducted as the new vicar of St Michael and all Angels church. For some reason, Ivy went to the occasion, presumably because Nancy asked her to come or because Jeffrey was singing in the choir. As she saw him process down the aisle, something happened inwardly that she could never describe or explain and she returned to church again. At first, she went only to Evensong and would not go to the morning service and receive Holy Communion. The priest came unexpectedly to see her and everything came flowing out after so many years. He listened without interruption before finally saying, "You blame God." Ivy realised that, of course, she had been blaming God, but had no idea that she was doing it. From that moment, everything improved for Ivy. She went to her first Confession and gradually became part of the church's life.

In 1978, Jeff by then was working in the Criminal Investigation Department (CID) of the Metropolitan Police. Without telling his mother, he used his contacts to seek out and discover where Richard John was buried. What happened next is recorded in her Spiritual Diary as follows.

30th January 1978

Today, my first child would have been 32 years old. I pray that he rests in peace, that although he never drew breath, yet he lived in my womb, and much has happened and been given to me because of him…My complete rejection of God for 16 years, because of the manner and deformity of his birth, yet God

21

continues to love even those who completely reject him and – if this is his will – draw them finally into his embrace…hope always, pray always for all others who have experienced a deep loss that they be led to him later as prayer and Christ heals. "Lord, show me thy face" he looked with compassion at the people who suffered, physically and mentally – "and he cast out devils." The sick in mind carry a great burden, one can be physically ill or deformed, yet remain mentally whole/alert, they may have learnt to come to terms with their disability and because of this are able to face life with courage, they are often happy and give much to others, nevertheless, there are many who are bitter and resentful and this will affect their mind, narrowing and warping it. It is whether they are able to accept the circumstances they find themselves in, acceptance brings peace within, fighting against the inevitable, often brings bitterness in its wake…' and he cast out devils' – Jesus the healer of minds…minds that are warped and twisted, unable to focus clearly, twisted by many forces of circumstance often outside their control. I am not going to attempt to explain the mind, I cannot anyway, it is enough to have learnt to recognise pain, to support them in their need, to encourage them to open up and talk it out, to be virtually unshakable, realising the extent of human suffering, keeping Christ continually in the centre of one's own life, to be open to the fact that we may be used for others, that Christ uses man for man, bringing an enrichment to one's life of love that comes before self, remaining God centred, drawing continuously from him – the well that never seems dry – giving everything back to Christ the giver, Christ heals, we do nothing in our own power…One's own faith can never be for oneself alone but must be deep enough and strong enough to sustain any number of people who may have no faith of their own or who have been so weakened that they have let go, to try to base one's own faith on the faith of Jesus in the Father, there is no distinction in Christ's healing of class or creed, there is no distinction in suffering either, being affluent brings no solace to the agony of mind whatever its origin might be…Healing begets healing, through the healing of self, one recognises the need in others! My mind returned to the woman who touched his robe 'and he felt the strength leave him', strength leaves one temporarily, but it is renewed again and again in him, he gave himself completely, to give oneself is to give all, it is not possible to give more than oneself, be prepared to be drained, retire at these moments into Christ, it is like dissolving oneself into his love, and in this, we are renewed. This is possible in any situation, during a one-one relationship, or in a crowded room, one withdraws inwardly to the light which is Christ and rests in it, while outwardly one continues with whatever the matter is in hand. This is given and understood in the continual practice of the presence of God. There are healers, psychiatrists, etc who themselves are overtaken by the ills of the world, perhaps through overwork, inability to relax, but mainly perhaps because after human strength fails, from whom do they draw? The healing Christ, compassionate, loving, also direct insomuch as he sees us without an outward facade, as we are, not as we would like others to see us, to heal, one must be aware of the whole real person as far as possible, the mind especially cannot be helped otherwise. One may be aware of healing gifts, in which case it would be false humility to play it down, so long as Christ remains always at the centre and is recognised as the giver. One may not be aware and there are many people who give so much without self-knowledge, but who are nevertheless healers…the ability to love, to put oneself alongside, to 'Be'.

(It is worth noting that at this time, Ivy is training to be a volunteer counsellor for the Samaritans, a role which she fulfils after training by being a member of staff at one of the charity's helpline call centres.)

30 August 1980

(Unbeknown to Ivy) Jeff has made enquiries and discovered the burial place of my first child, not in Queen's Road (cemetery) but Chingford (cemetery). At the time it happened January 1946, I refused to listen when the undertaker told me, I was very distraught and disturbed, but as I have written earlier, I believe the death and consequent suffering made a deep impact and was indeed the beginning of my spiritual life that I was subsequently led to, the soul of a stillborn child…it has lived within the womb…one-minute particle of the 'lights of heaven' – forever with the Father – This was Jeffrey's quest, not mine, he said, "I have always thought of him as your baby…he is also my brother." How these thoughts infiltrate into the mind, and what grows from them!

8 September

I went with Jeff's wife and elder son to Chingford Mount Cemetery and we were given directions by the Superintendent and so found the grave of my first child…a stillborn son whose name would have been Richard John. Inwardly, I was moved far more deeply than I would have thought possible…something returned crystal clear in my mind, I remember picking my grandson up and holding him tightly! Since then, my thoughts have constantly returned to this child...that he now has his place in heaven as an infant light, I have no doubts...A definite purpose has been served regarding me...he is, as Ron said to me, "Our own flesh and blood." I imagined as I looked at his place of burial...his little malformed body committed to the earth, and my reaction at the time – my total and complete rejection of him. By the grace of God, I have been led and guided over the years, and have been enabled to understand the purpose of it all, through suffering comes love. This has been painful for me. But the difference, I suppose, is that now, I do accept it and offer it to God. I no longer withdraw, but face it, it has happened, it is part of my life, and through it, I have learned. Last Friday, to DT, it was a great help to be able to talk the above out with him.

10 September

Prayer – Spiritual Communion, the approaching light entered...later I thought about this...Why was it withheld? Is it to ensure that faith is understood? The thought turned to the soul – It may be likened to a bed of many flowers – buds are meant to open fully and to bloom! Later, my thoughts were on the word "rejection." No doubt, it has entered at this point because of 'Richard John'. It bears reflection.

11 September

Attended the Mass, various thoughts were in my mind, but I feel empty and very tired...We reject that which contains a flaw. That which is not perfect we reject, also that with which we are unable to cope – that which disturbs us – that which has hurt us. Quite a long time ago, a priest said to me regarding a difficult relationship, "You have not rejected her"...but he was wrong. I went through the outward motions, yes – but within my heart, I had rejected her...all this was later healed but only after much heart-searching and pain, and only after trying to see one's own self in truth...not an easy thing to do, we see what we wish to see! So we reject what has given us pain...we shut out in order to escape. This may be necessary at the time in order to try and preserve oneself...one builds a wall of self-protection. This sort of rejection does not only reject the person the situation etc...it is blind to the presence within its own soul of Our Lord – and of the love and healing power contained therein – when through the receiving of the Sacraments and prayer we are opened...healing may begin healing of oneself, often a slow and painful process. It is not difficult to apportion blame, and it is not difficult to blame God! When we are ready to acknowledge what is within ourselves, then we are on the road. This does not mean we have not suffered pain, it means that in the recognition of it and the offering of it, it is no longer negative, but used to effect complete healing...the inner eye begins to perceive Christ present in that which was rejected.

21 September

Ron and I went to our first baby's grave today, I am at peace now concerning it all...we tidied it up and tomorrow Jeff's wife and I will do with the shears and do it properly. I have a plant to put on and in October – November's time, Ron will put some roses in. Somehow, all this has brought me much closer to Richard John...and I recognise God's purpose. Mass this morning, and within my mind, the empty Cross of the Risen Christ! Later I realised something else, it is not only the discovery and visiting of the grave of my child but the sudden realisation that now I am praying for him.

17 November

Ron and I went to Richard John's grave yesterday and planted some bulbs and a rose tree. I wonder what Ron is thinking, it was his suggestion we go, and although I know it is only "little bones," yet I am drawn closer and closer to this child.

24 December

In prayer, within intercession to the Holy Mother was received again holding the infant Christ...the marks of crucifixion upon him, immediately from this came thoughts of my first-born son...and from this came prayer for all mothers and all children in need!

1981

24 January

Ron and my 38th wedding anniversary, how fortunate we have been, in so many ways (laughter) we do realise how the years have flown, and who can say what is left, but there are no regrets, we live one day at a time. (The value of the present moment) We went to Richard John's grave today, he would have been 35 years old on 30 January. The rose cutting Ron planted has taken – he does have green fingers – the crocuses are peeping through, neither of us finds anything morbid in this…as I have already written, I feel so close to this child, there is peace in the knowledge that his purpose has borne fruit…

26 January

Thoughts again of 'Richard John' and the importance of living within the womb, it goes no further than this yet, just that it is so…

23 August

Ron and I went to tend the grave, we do not go too often, just to keep it presentable, the rose cuttings have taken well, actually, there is no sense of morbidity at all, in fact, I always feel peace there…as I watched Ron, a mental picture of Aunty (Nancy Pickett) came to me, the last time I saw her, her haunted eyes "will it be all right…are you sure…how do you know?" and my thoughts came gently, all is indeed well.

30 August

I was very touched when Jeff showed me a cross he has made for Richard John's grave, I would like the word 'fruition' put on it, for that is exactly what it is…I am surprised when traits appear in people, and one has little idea that they are present.

1982

30 May

Ron and I took some more earth to the grave – one pink rose was in full bloom – it still needed more earth after two years. I find much comfort in the stillness…there are no disturbing thoughts, only knowledge that in God, all is made well.

(Richard John never became for Ivy, a shaman or spiritual guide, rather she realised that his purpose in being conceived and carried in her womb during his

short life was now being fulfilled in his ministry of prayer in heaven among the holy innocents.)

Returning to Ivy's spiritual journey after her return to church as a communicant, her growth in faith and practice developed in the following way.

In 1962, she met D.B.T. but it was not until 1967, the year in which he was priested, she began to really know him as a person in a friendship which lasted to the end of her life. In 1969, she went to her first retreat at Hemingford Grey and she said of it, "I took to it like a duck to water." She became a lay member of the Community of the Resurrection in Yorkshire, (where incidentally D.B.T. trained at its theological college), through the retreat house at Hemingford Grey which was run by the community. A series of spiritual directors from the community took her on at their East London house, The Royal Foundation of St Katherine, Stepney, the last being Fr Reginald Smith CR, who on being recalled to the Mother House, led to D.B.T. taking on this role for her. After a period of a few years, in December 1975, she heard Martin Israel preach at St Michael's Walthamstow and later went to a Quiet Day led by him at St Edward's House, Westminster. She recognised that this was the person who would be her director in the future and so it proved to be.

We have now come to the point where we can move forward in the next chapter to discover through Ivy's writings in her Spiritual Diary and Martin's letters to her and how their relationship developed, changed and deepened, as he influenced her and she influenced him. This continued until his death in 2007. Ivy had moved to Holbeach in Lincolnshire in 1999 and found a new and good life, while still keeping in touch with Martin Israel and D.B.T. However, her health declined until she was unable to keep herself safe at home and her sons, with her consent, found her a care home in Spalding where she could be looked after. Unfortunately, it was a women's only care home and Ivy found the other women were often catty towards one another and the conversation usually shallow. Her room was small but looked out on a pretty garden and she gradually remained in her room more and more until she remained there the entire time. Also, she became more and more obsessed about the date of her death and would point to the metal cross above her bed and ask why he would not take her. The last passages in her Spiritual Diary in the summer of 2008, speak of this increasing concern of hers that she had outlived her usefulness and desired to go. It was an intensification of a trend in her life dating back to her early life, when she was quite convinced that she would die on 30 September 1994. The date came and went and nothing happened but the concern in her mind remained until she died, supported by Christopher and Jeffrey, at the care home on 17 July 2012. Her funeral was in Spalding church, and her ashes were buried in the churchyard of Holbeach church. Her wish was to have them scattered in the nothingness of the mouth of the River Nene as it enters The Wash was not fulfilled. Changes in the law limited the disposal of ashes to specified places designated for them such as consecrated ground.

Chapter 2
Martin Israel and Ivy Goodley
(1976–2007) 1976

21 January

Have telephoned DT as I cannot get to the Martin Israel retreat.

Ivy has heard of him and asked me if I thought she should go to one of his retreats. I agreed that this would be a good thing to do. Eventually, she found a place at one of his quiet days later in the year.

5 July

I went last Saturday to St Edward's House, Westminster for a quiet day, the conductor was Dr Martin Israel. He is an unusual-looking man, not attractive, rather compelling but he was so good, right off the cuff. The vicar told me he is going to conduct a retreat for us, perhaps next year, although he has a church (Cornhill), he travels around a great deal, also through this quiet day, I straightened things out between (X) and myself. I have so much to learn, things I thought I had – I have not – but I have known (X) for such a long time, I am glad all is well between us.

Ivy's confessor Fr Reginald Smith CR, had recently been recalled to Mirfield, leaving her without a successor and her mind is clearly turning towards asking Martin Israel to take her on. She writes to him after the quiet day to ask him if he would be willing to do so.

20 July

On my return (from a holiday in Somerset) I received a letter from Dr Martin Israel, he is willing to accept me and be my confessor/director, he wants me to visit him at Kensington on 18 August, this is wonderful, so much is given to me. It will be somebody completely outside of all people and relationships that I have, and I feel at this stage is what I need. I shall have to phone DT before he goes on holiday and talk it out, I shall have to tell Dr Israel about him, but it must make no difference to our relationship.

26 July

DT rang, he is very pleased by Dr Israel's acceptance, which brings me peace, a prayer of thanks to God for all things.

When Ivy called me to say that Martin Israel had accepted her, I predicted that the day would come sooner rather than later, that he would depend upon her as much as she would depend upon him. It would be a relationship of equals. In the beginning, this was not so, but it rapidly grew to be so. Note the change after the first meeting when Ivy stops calling him Doctor and begins calling him Father. It then moves on beyond that and we can see the movement towards equality in the changing relationship between them, as evidenced below. So far, the relationship has moved on to that of confessor/director. Later, it moves on to become more mutual, as is shown by the meetings recorded below. There is plenty of material available from later meetings to exemplify this change. In the opening quotations, Ivy uses the letter X when she does not want to refer to another person openly in her spiritual diary but she soon drops this device in favour of using initials instead, as less confusing. For example, I, myself, am called friend, D or DT or DBT.

6 August

I have been thinking a bit about Dr Israel and DT, that friendship and love will continue with DT but my spiritual life must necessarily be in the hands of Dr Israel, within I know this, I also realise that in being able to do this I have achieved detachment.

A day or two before 18 August.

Ivy is making notes on a passage in St John of the Cross and writes:

At this point – and not for DT – I intend to talk to Dr Israel, although I do believe that DT has been an excellent director (leaving personal friendship and love aside), I cannot see when it involves his own personal life, that he can be detached enough to advise me correctly.

19 August

My visit to Fr Israel yesterday was obviously so right, what a wonderful man he is. Many things were talked about, from my earliest family history to my present spiritual life, he has met DT and although I had not mentioned surnames he said, "You have been totally honest with me, so I am going to be honest with you, I have met him." He told me where, he said, "you must give him all the love you can, you must strengthen him and support him at all times, and when the break comes, as it will come—you must be there to uphold him, he is to be your life's work so that, ultimately he will be fulfilled in the (......) of his vocation." During confession, he again said, "You must love him unreservedly and without judgment. You are well along the road." He laid his hands upon my head, with pressure, he did not speak, it seemed to go on for a long time and then he said, "let us say together the Lord's Prayer." Afterwards, he said, "let us pray silently together." As I left he took my hands, he said, "Our relationship will be very fruitful," spiritually he said, "There is nothing at the moment for me to say except be still in God." I see him next at his church on 28 September, he says he understands the love I have for DT, it is not mother love, neither is it the love of a man and a woman, later he explained it all to me. I know I have received a great blessing in being given this man, I know he will lead me, and I know it is right.

29 September

Although I have to go through with all Fr M.I. has said, I feel a little apprehensive. I hope there will not be a bad reaction, and one must just proceed in faith. Much of what Fr M.I. said of himself, and my general impression of him, has made me think a great deal about him. I wrote the following lines concerning him without fully understanding.

'Gentle man, falling softly as flowered petal upon earth, Touching each blade and leaf with silver thread,

Lightly as a maiden's dance – an infant kiss –
So falls the rain,
So falls a tear for thee.'

When I write to him concerning (DT's) reaction after next Friday, I shall send these lines to him. I think I probably do understand without wishing to put it into words.

30 September

Later I went to church, nobody was there. I knelt in the Lady Chapel. God knew what was in my heart and into my understanding came the words, "Have I not told you? All shall be well." I smiled, 'Lord.'

2 October

Yesterday I went to see (DT). All my apprehensions had gone and I knew that what I experienced in the Lady Chapel was so right. We talked for a long time, at one point (DT) said, "All this last hour or more is God, isn't it? God – God." Of course, it is God, nothing of our relationship would have happened at all if God had not been at the centre. I have no doubts now that Fr M.I. will become (crossed out) in the foreseeable future and this is very necessary because of what lies before (DT).

6 October

Fr M.I.'s book arrived from Mowbray's, 'Precarious Living'. At a glance through it, I see it shows the man and his journey to the priesthood and his other life's work...Having read about a third of the book, the first thing that impresses itself on my mind is the 'finger of God was upon him', and once this is so with any person, then one follows the will of God, often the lonely path, but also the path of love and joy. How truly blessed are they who have been touched by the finger of God, 'you have not chosen me but I have chosen you'...Back into my mind came something I felt I should do regarding Fr. M.I. the last time I saw him – the Kiss of Peace? Of all things of the understanding concerning him, also in some stranger way, of something he has missed...From the Cloud of Unknowing, 'by love may be gotten and holden, by thought never'. That Fr M.I. has travelled the road of loneliness and great suffering, that in middle age he was priested, yet despite what he says, I do not think the loneliness and suffering is his past – one part of it is past but had come to the point of priesthood – in another way it will begin again, further than that I cannot say, because I do not know, it is something within the loneliness of the true celibate priest…one other thing from his book which I have now finished, 'the mother', not what he says, but what he does not say, too deep for the public eye of all and sundry that may read this very moving and biographical part of the book – I find here and very great suffering.

15 December

I saw Fr M.I., first the picture I gave him 'Souvenir d'Ttalie', he knew immediately what it was, he said, "It means so much to me, it is an answer to prayers. I shall put it in my meditation room in my little country place. What do you see in it?"

I said, "You, freedom of spirit."

He repeated, "It means so much to me at this time."

We spoke of love, he said he was attracted to me, otherwise, he would not have accepted me, and that there were many forms of love that did not involve going to bed. He experienced this with his students and others. We looked at each other. I said, "I see great loneliness."

"Yes," he said, "It will always be with me, there are only one or two people that understand me. I still wonder why God has allowed me to be, what is me?"

I said, "I wondered this about myself."

He said, "You have been blessed, and you have a very high degree of mysticism, there is no direction I am going to give you, it is a shared relationship, continue as you are, enter into the stillness of mind-heart, as often as you can, you have told me what I would have said – spiritual insight."

(From now on, Martin's title Father' is dropped and he is simply called Martin Israel or M.I.)

1977

6 December

I went to see M.I, we are so in tune. We discussed my spiritual life, and the pieces I write he says are wonderful! Advice regarding certain things which are very helpful, and confirmation on other issues. We talked about X and his reaction. I felt very sorry for M.I., he is a lonely man, he said, "I am alone but I have the Lord." I do hope that eventually he and D.T. will become friends, I know he wishes it, if God wills it – then it shall be. I asked him for direction regarding this particular issue. I feel that if I cannot assure M.I. that his personal confidences will not go from me to D.T., then on a spiritual level he may close up and this would be wrong for him, it means that I shall have to carry his secret. I wish to share with M.I. I need an ear. (He) said, "Let us lay it before God now and see what we are given."

He put the light out! I was aware only of X before the crucifix, that I must give away on this, he is alone and require total confidence from me, and that I would only talk to M.I. regarding X intimate matters if it was essential to me and that I really couldn't cope, he earlier suggested that I, in fact, tell a lie, but I refused to do this, I looked at him and said, "But it would be a lie." I cannot go against the truth, neither can I deliberately lie. This does show a definite weakness in M.I., it is the second time it has happened, but it does not make any difference to me regarding him, I just understand it. He asked me to say first what I was given in prayer (above). He was given something quite different, that at any time and at all times he is there if X needs his help. So in fact, God gave me my answer definitively in that prayer. M.I. gave me no direction but accepted what I said. Later, he told me of a paper going around for signatures to allow men to live together in peace if they wish to, that he had signed this and believed they must be free to choose their way of life…That he would have to answer for it in certain quarters, to tell X this if I wished, but to make sure that he did not mean this in any patronising manner.

He said, "I have a great respect for him, perhaps love is a strong word." He goes to West Mailing this coming weekend! He spoke off the cuff, regarding the hopes of a former Archbishop of Canterbury – there are so few people one can trust and that he had misjudged others, others who he was sure he could trust but learnt that they had betrayed him, in so many devious ways.

This talk helped me considerably, keeping my own counsel. I left him, saying to him, "All shall be well." I felt sorrow because, because of what I saw, and certain things he said, he agreed with me that celibates lack something vital in comparison with one who runs the whole gamut of human emotions, that one is called completely to God in whatever area of life we are. He said there is no difference. I said I had 'seen' something concerning him, that he would give up his work to the full-time ministry.

He said with no surprise, "It is what I want to do."

1978

28 February

Today I went to see M.I., his remarks regarding X made me laugh. "I know there are great depths there but he looks so insignificant, something should be done about his appearance, etc. I answered him by saying, "If you ever get the opportunity, ask him to take his glasses off, then you will see the depth'…he looked amazed! Many other things were discussed, he asked if all that I wrote was recorded, and I said it was, he said it was important to do this, nothing must be lost. I told him all would go eventually to D.T. spiritually, he again said my progress was amazing. It is strange at these times, I feel completely detached, and as though it was somebody else he was talking about. Finally, we prayed together. I at once was in-depth, the crucifix in the light? I heard him say, "Amen." He said, this was a deep meditation, a very deep meditation." He did not ask me what, neither did he say of himself, this is how it is with him. I feel I am as one. Later in prayer, the crucifix in light, 'This is my body', do this!

23 May

(After a distressing morning concerned with parish affairs, Ivy visits M.I.)

I really do feel detached from it all as he speaks to me of what I write, he says they are Divine Revelations and it is wonderful, etc. He could not read the last one I sent to him quickly enough. I talked to him about the line in my Father's house are many mansions', he says he is longing to read it. I shall send it before I go into retreat, then I can go in and see him about it. It really is a detached feeling, there is certainly nothing emotional. I feel very quiet about it all. Nevertheless, we did have a good talk about this and I do find him not only understanding but reassuring. He has written a new book, called, I think, 'The Holy Spirit'. He also talked of further revelations given to himself through which he has been freed from many things. We discussed all sorts of things, he says he loves Pleshey! And is looking forward immensely to going there. He returned later to prayer life, and we spent about 20 minutes in complete silence. He said it is wonderful to share these times together, but I had no thought of this myself. I found it quite difficult to come out of this depth because I suppose I was brought out of it, it did not finish naturally. There is a definite rapport between us at these times. I am very aware of it, yet I am also aware of a barrier that I think comes from me. I sense he is very lonely. I listen but do not respond as I ought to.

9 June

Today I go to Pleshey in retreat. Conducted by M.I. I am sure it will prove a wonderful time and that yet another turning point in my life…I do not know why I have put this but I feel it strongly. Thoughts return to M.I. and I see the same now as I remember seeing right at the beginning – defencelessness, vulnerability. As far as I am concerned, all is very gentle. Fr M.I. really is a very quiet man and as he says, he really does not have any small talk. I feel it rather tends to make people a little uncomfortable, but there it is, it is just not in him…He is a naturally gifted speaker; it flows easily from him.

Meditation, he read from the Gospels, the woman at the well, after which we meditated upon it or dismissed it, etc, as we would. Once or twice I opened my eyes, each time there was a little smile around his mouth as if he was 'seeing' something beautiful. Later I went to see him, he said he has received much from God himself this weekend, that his medical practice must continue, at least until he is definitely shown otherwise, and that within himself he is now truly celibate, and that because of this point that he has reached, he is to be shown more and more of God…I find his words "within myself, I am now truly celibate" at first glance at them surprising, but on a little reflection I understand…one may be married and yet be spiritually truly celibate. In his room it was so still, he looks so happy, no doubt about what he has received.

30 November

Yesterday, I went to M.I.'s. Although what he said about the relationship between us was not a surprise to me, nevertheless it felt rather strange to hear him say it, that he was not a spiritual director as such to me, but that he saw me as a friend and companion, that we would share our personal thoughts at every level, and talk about spiritual things at depth. He spoke of love and said he was not ashamed to use that word although there were no carnal thoughts, I think at this point my face had become poker-faced. Although I understand perfectly what he meant, I wonder rather why he felt he must put it into words'! I said to him, "Love is a much-misused word." He then went on to talk a great deal about himself…his spiritual life at the moment…the 'message' from a nun now passed on, to pray without ceasing for the Nazis and his own views on this as a Jew turned Christian, his place in Sussex (Robertsbridge) which incidentally Ron and I pass through on our way to Hastings, his prayer life, his work, difficulties here, his unattained as yet call to a full-time ministry, his father, South Africa, his favourite retreat house in Pleshey, personal matters that I shall not write here, although I understood to a point, his opinion of me which rather embarrassed me…many, many things I said to him, "God does work in a mysterious way." He nodded and smiled, "who he brings together." Actually, on reflection of all this, of his position etc, I do not feel afraid, only rather wonder at God and accept it all as from Him. It feels right and I am sure much will follow on now. He has made our position clear. The piece I wrote in September while on holiday in Norfolk for him, although I sent it to him, I did not tell him it was for him. It has all materialised. I give thanks to Almighty God for all he has given me. We had about 15 minutes of silent prayer together at the end, telephone off the hook, light out…I had discussed with him my thoughts on the Holy Mother, which I received in prayer twice during this last week, I felt sure about writing them down. During this silent prayer together it immediately returned, so I write it as directed, a series of mental pictures. The Holy Mother with the dead body of her Son…anguish…she is led away by St John to whom Jesus has given her…there is nothing further to do with the Holy Mother at this point…there follows light…a soul travelling towards eternity…stillness, inner stillness as one rests in the light. Our Lord ascending to the Father, bearing within his heart the soul of his Mother. Together, they enter the light of eternity. I cannot describe the beauty here…not beauty of anything 'seen', but beauty in awareness of love, a complete merging of Triune love, at the receiving by the Father of the soul of Mary contained within the heart of the Son.

1979

11 March

Received a letter from M.I., he says of DT that there is an important ecclesiastical future…not spiritual future, and how sad that the two cannot be equated! I am going to question him on this next time I see him…only time will tell, of course…and God's will in the matter may well be true…but, are there ecclesiastical greats who are also spiritual men?

(There turned out to be no important ecclesiastical future for DT, as for his spiritual future, that is not assessable.).

24 April

Referring back to one of M.I.'s letters, again he has foreseen something that is now materialising in this relationship with Fr Bebbington (former vicar of St Michael and All Angels, Walthamstow). Talk on the phone too with DT. I am concerned for his health…the stress under which he is living is taking its toll. He now has a hospital appointment, how long is he going to be able to stand this pressure? How long should he? I am very concerned for him.

23 May

I met M.I. today, he talked at length regarding his work. He showed me a letter which he said was typical, asking for his help over the power of evil. He treats me as an equal, but I know that I am not…a great deal is over my head…he is finding it hard work…draining…yet he is immersed in it and would not free himself if he could we talked at length of many subjects…he refers to my latest writing as "Revelations," he said, which made me laugh (inwardly), regarding the hereafter of which I have just written, "I do not think you or I will have to go through that, there is nothing in our lives that merits that, except that I know, I do not love enough." Well, I wish I could be as sure as he is, in fact, I believe every soul must go through it, there are many inward facets of us all that must be purified before the journey in the flame can continue, but I said nothing other than about his reference to Pleshey in July. His remarks regarding the West Mailing I am sure are not too flattering, but I think many people are rather frightened of the depth which he (sees) and at his reference to evil too, which I am sure he is being called upon to deal with…but as he says, people do not understand his thoughts…he said he does not want me to have to deal with this yet…I do not think in this context at the moment…whether I shall be led into, this remains to be seen (7 July 1982). I feel much more at ease having been able to unload on him, it is not that he advises, he rarely does this, but it does me a great deal of good to talk it all out, and I know I must follow what I have been shown, if the way becomes harder, I must be stronger.

16 July

Arrived at Pleshey in good time, it is good to be with M.I. for a little talk it seemed he was anxious to tell me about his meeting (with another priest whom he knew). I said that in a practical sense there was nothing I could do, but I would continue my prayer unremittingly for him, that I had for a long time used the Holy Mother to intercede for him, it is strange, for a long time I have prayed for his priesthood, his ministry, and his service to God, etc. I said to M.I. that he did possess great inner strength. Well, I have much to pray about in this retreat.

"This conversation seems at first to be a serious breach of confidentiality on the part of M.I. but later in the diary, it seems clear that the priest did give him permission to speak to her and when they met, he was happy that the conversation had taken place."

17 July

The retreat is to be on the inner life. "Mass that M.I. conducts with love…Having been in to see him, regarding me," he says it is the true spiritual life…he uses the word non-attachment in preference to detachment…there is love, prayer, and availability, of course, I am concerned – yet above this and beyond this is peace…it touches me, yet I am not touched, it sounds contradictory, it is difficult to put into words, he understands because it is how he is himself, and far more so than I am.

18 July

I was rather surprised yesterday when I saw M.I. at his reference to suicide, how near he had been to contemplating it…before he made the decision, that the suffering and the darkness had been so intense that death seemed welcoming…but his call upon God that saved him…

19 July

The retreat finishes after breakfast tomorrow, it has been a good retreat, the addresses remain one hour long, it flows from M.I. like a brook. Some things I do not approve of, e.g. his reference to certain clergy he knows who do not know how to pray. True, I'm sure, but not necessary to say it publicly. He is a strange man in many ways, in our private talk he did speak for the first time of his mother, her complete possession of him, body and mind, but he said, "Fortunately, she died when I was a young man." His two elderly women friends with whom he does most of his intercessory prayer – one is of Quaker origin, one is a Spiritualist, neither of them goes to church, but both are women of love. He recognises their failure, but they are great intercessors. Again, he spoke of evil…things he will never be able to publicise…and the work he feels called upon to do in this sphere…he is totally single-minded…and so unattached that I doubt if any person means a great deal to him, although obviously he feels drawn to certain people. I feel he has missed out on much in life, but at the same time, this is his road and he has recognised it. I do feel drawn to him in certain ways, but his road is not mine. At supper tonight, I sat directly behind Fr M.I. and spent the time meditating upon the back of his head, wondering about its 'contents'! One thing in the last address registered. He said that whatever we have built up and accomplished within ourselves in this life will be taken with us into the next and into eternity! So material gain, possessions drop from us at death.

(A little while later, Ivy, in a telephone conversation with M.I. brings up the subject of priests who do not know how to pray being mentioned in a retreat address and tells him that she does not think it right. Her words were, "It is not worthy of you." He responds, "Truth spoken in love" and *accepts* this.)

23 August

After what M.I. told me, I felt rather worried but all appears to be well. I can only think that DT was right, M.I. has no conception of married life, and has read into it more than was there. (When I met him), I laughed and said, "I know who you have been talking to, it works both ways you know." Nothing further was said and obviously, he is not going to discuss M.I., but I have a strong suspicion that he knows that I know. All seems well.

13 September

Yesterday I went to see M.I. we talked about many things, he asked me my reaction to Walsingham last time. I said there had been no change and I literally could not wait to get on the coach, nevertheless, at DT's request, I was still going with them in early October. (See below on 9 October) Well, M.I. had visited Walsingham deliberately in August, he had exactly the same reaction as myself, but on a deeper and more psychic level…he was rather disturbed at this, so contacted the vicar of St James's Piccadilly without telling him that he himself had been and asked his reaction which was exactly the same, so he said to my inward amusement, "that is three of us." Actually, he has put into words what I felt and it has given me relief of mind. I thought I had created a block but he said, "No I had not." This in no way takes away anything that others receive there. He, in his psychic power, senses evil, this is a strong word and not one I would use personally, but in this respect, he is on a far deeper plane than I am. I shall go now in October with a restful mind. On the writing I have sent him, he has the same reaction as DT and moved to tears, he says it is not finished yet! What he is receiving is running parallel to mine, but he did not enlarge on it, and I am glad of this…He again emphasised DT as my work and I am the one, etc. A great deal on this was said, but I have no need of this now. I have realised the depth of the words, "Lead gently by the still waters of love." (West Mailing)

He was immensely pleased with the stole. He is like a little boy and cannot open the parcel quick enough but I have given it for a reason, inner prompting, and much will come of this…all in all, very worthwhile.

9 October

Last weekend to Walsingham with DT and parish, apart from the beginning when I felt very uptight, it was a lovely weekend. I still don't particularly want to go, certainly not for a long time, nevertheless much good came from it. Firstly, DT's priestly role. So much love and care for his people, it emanated from him and the priesthood was there for all to see and receive from. I realised literally quite suddenly how important the Priesthood is and how it must be protected at all costs. This is his true vocation, it came over loud and clear. Secondly, I met and talked to one of the parishioners who has a son of 19 years with cerebral palsy (who) came with us. He is totally unable to do anything at all for himself; we talked at great length, sharing spiritually as well. She lives off the Royal Mews and has asked me to visit, so on 5 November I shall go when (DT) takes their communion and take it from there. I never think these meetings are accidental but are for a reason and meant to be used.

19 December

Today. I went to M.I.'s, much was talked about, including most unexpectedly his offer to conduct a Blessing for (X). This is right out of the blue, I have no idea of either of them reacting to this, but as he said it is love…somewhere along the line I reminded him of the line received at West Mailing "Lead gently by the still waters of love." Many times, this line penetrates my thought. He asked about Christmas, I said it would be a family time in Bristol, etc. He said briefly, "I am visiting my father in South Africa." That was all. We finished with silent prayer as always, telephone off the hook, light out. To my inward vision came the infant crucified, the crucifixion of innocence. I held this and was appalled inwardly at the depth of suffering I was made aware of. This was followed immediately by a mental picture of M.I. (the son) and his father. I said to him after he had put the light on, "What I received was strange, shall I tell you?" "Yes," he said, so I did, saying afterwards "It is you, isn't it?" He replied, "It has always been so, my father is the reason that I am celibate today and why I have always been celibate." He looked at me and asked, "Must I go?" I replied, "Yes, you must go." He spoke a little of the difficulties and I do realise the depth of these, but this will probably be the culmination of it all, he will receive all he needs to get through this. "All shall be well." I felt a depth within me responding to the suffering of this man. As I left, I kissed him on the cheek. I could sense that he was momentarily caught off-balance, but he responded and did likewise. I wonder how long since this has happened to him, I felt he needed it, he asked for my prayers. I shall pray.

M.I.'s own prayer at this time had been intercession to the Holy Mother to intercede on his behalf during his visit "home." Regarding retreat next year, he says I do not need a conducted retreat and suggests I make a private retreat at Bumham Abbey. He appears to hold this place in high spiritual esteem as opposed to West Mailing, where he says it is a nice place to visit...he finds nothing there!

21 January 1980

I had a letter from Burnham Abbey, a very nice letter from Sister Raphael Mary, M.I. is her director too. I am glad to have been told this...So I shall make a private retreat there 20–23 May.

11 March

To M.I.'s today, had a long interesting spiritual talk, he again likened me to Mother Julian of Norwich, "Not," he said, "to boost me," but that it is what he thought when I first went to him almost four years ago. He says the writing is important and will get more so, it is strange to me that as each lot ends, I cannot think there can be more to come but there is. His visit to his father at Christmas was very successful.

He said, "I have waited 25 years for this." He spoke of internal suffering, he is writing another book on this subject. He made me laugh, he says, "I am earthy!" When I asked exactly what he meant, he said, "Your feet are on the earth." I said that within my mind this last couple of days during prayer, there had been stones. "Large or small?" he asked.

"Large," I said.

"Good," apparently the small ones have little meaning. During our prayer together, this clarified little rock-like stones before the entrance into the tomb! Afterwards, he gave me a blessing, I could feel warmth filling me, and he said something important might be given to me (spiritual). He also said how close we are spiritually, there are things that can be said to each other, one could not on a spiritual level say to another person, we spoke also of detachment, I am more and more aware of spiritual growth I know, but it is good to be reassured on this point. I never cease to be amazed at the people God brings to each other. There was talk on other people too, but not to be written here.

30 May

Later to DT, I had a lovely relaxing time. We talked of my will that I shall shortly make…these spiritual diaries, he must do as he likes. I know M.I.'s views on them. The personal mementoes I shall leave him to speak of, what is nearest my heart, my crucifix and chain (some words crossed out) and money for a chasuble, the (Two words crossed out) speaks of…an unbroken circle from here into eternity our friendship…the love in which it is rooted…there is no need to say more.

5 June

Yesterday I went to see M.I. much was talked out. He thinks my name should be used in any publication that might be after my death; he asked me why I was against this and I could only think it was pride, but he did not agree, so I must bring this up again with DT. Hopefully, between now and my death M.I. and DT will get to know each other better, I hope it happens as I think he could be a great help to DT over sifting through the writings, and it is what he wants to do anyway but nothing must be forced. It is rather off-putting to sit facing him and be told I am a spiritual director and on a par with Mother Julian of Norwich. Fortunately, much is removed from me and it has no effect on me, nevertheless! I find it difficult to believe; it passes from me. We discussed our respective way of prayer. In many ways, our approach is identical (M.I. and myself). It is always good to talk to him. In silent prayer at the end was immediate recollection and travelling to the Seventh Veil, again the division of the streams…the centre stream upon which no souls, flows within the inner 'eye' to the Father whence it comes…this is the stream of living water issuing from the Father through the Son into the world. This is the water from the pierced side of Christ and from which appeared so many springs. It is the living bridge to the Father…of the eternal, piercing the 'merging' of both worlds…it is the stream of life that feeds the heavens and the earth…the inward 'eye' is upon the centre stream in the Seventh Veil. It is water but there is no sense of a flowing, no movement. It appears as crystal…unfathomable depth…the well of the Son, rooted in the Creator…silence. Our eyes met and I knew that he understood.

8 June

I have been thinking over what M.I. said regarding using my name and have asked four people close to me, three are for using it, one is not…I wonder why M.I. is so for it? Thoughts entered my head regarding this, I am still not for it, or else just to use my middle name "Margaret" which would not mean anything to people…will ask what A's own opinion is and probably be guided by that.

3 July

The one picture concerning M.I. remains unchanged, he kneels at a Prie Dieu, he rises and makes his way to an altar, and it does not appear to be a high altar…There is nothing further, it is always the same. When I saw him last, I told him this, he looked at me very intently and said it is tied up with his own spiritual way, and we would see now it has gone further within myself, he is fully robed as to conduct mass, he approaches the altar which had not changed, it is a small altar, but the light is radiant upon it, there is the exposition of the Blessed Sacrament, he prostrates himself before it, yet I am aware it is in such great humility and devotion that a chord is touched, there is a knowledge present that there is a 'calling' from Our Blessed Lord that will concern him deeply…this too has repeated itself in prayer several times.

9 July

A repetition regarding M.I., again it proceeds a little further, everything is as before, he takes the monstrance within his hands and turns, there are no people present…yet he holds it forth…this appears to be a sign of his acceptance? It fades.

10 July

I have begun to write the story of my life, I am absorbed, memories come flooding back, so fresh and clear…Mass this morning…peace. I asked to be shown God's will for me…how he wishes me to serve him…

27 December

M.I. "What you felt called upon to write to your father did have an effect on him, even subconsciously and not admitted by him, nevertheless it would be absorbed and held, more especially perhaps because unknown to either of you, he was close to death, so entering eternity with it." All indeed is well.

1981

11 April

My 63rd birthday! on the phone, to my director, he asked my opinion of the retreat he has done before, so after having asked to make sure it was all right to say exactly what I thought, I did tell him of something he always says regarding clergy that I am sure would be better left unsaid, as I said to him, "You are worth more than that."

He said, "Truth in love" and that is what it is, although I would not have told him unasked.

28 April

I have written the following for my director on his 54th birthday…30 April.
"What is time, my friend?"
Other than a long and often tortuous road that we must travel…
Here and there a place to rest…
At the well perchance a kindred soul to lighten us…To bind our wounds…
Even to accompany us as we tread the unknown…

Of times lonely is the path and dark the horizon

…brave the elements,

Pressing ever forward to the known goal, presenting itself in the darkness of faith…

"When naught shall be 'seen' within but light,

And naught 'known' but God."

30 April

A friend from St Michael's phoned to tell me that Fr Geoffrey Curtis C.R. died early today. I do know how great a help he was, and a friend too, to my director. I know how greatly he will miss him, how strange it should be on his (M.I.) birthday. Later, I reread the above that I had sent to him…it could have been himself to Fr Curtis! I telephoned him!

1 May

Prayer…intercession…within the intercession to the Holy Mother the knowledge of Fr M.I. returned clearly, it was always in a state of supplication…it has not changed for a long time, he approaches the tabernacle and holds forth the Host…with this comes clearly within the words, "My son, I have need of thee." I do not know what this implies, only that there is something being asked of him that he is not doing?

28 May

Have nearly finished Fr M.I. latest book 'The pain that heals'. I think there is repetition, much that has been previously written, but it is in great depth…I do find much of his writing "dark" as opposed to talking to him. I feel within him something almost unfathomable.

4 June

Went to see my director…We talked much out. I am still always inwardly surprised at some things to do with him personally, but I realise I must learn to get myself out of the way completely and be ready to be used as God wishes me to be. We had little time for silent prayer at the end this time, but in the time there was came clearly the line again "My son, I have need of thee." this had been talked about previously between us as to its meaning, to my understanding, it means the whole of himself to be consecrated to God…the whole one would have said that the whole was already given…I am sure he will be led to it. It was very good to be able to unload certain things…I asked him regarding Mother Julian, and he thinks this is the right time for me to read it properly. I do feel very strongly about it, drawing more and more to it…with reference to his book 'The pain that heals', he is giving me a copy. I shall read it again, but more slowly. I told him about the 'dark' that I find in his writing as opposed to talking to him. I have had further insight on this…the 'dark' is the darkness of pain that is like a well within him, that is released in his writing…the repetition I have referred to is the deepening levels of pain that rise again and again, and are not finished yet…the 'light' that one sees when talking with him is the result of the release within him…the gradual release within him from the darkness of suffering, that manifests itself in his teaching, through all this is shown his own growth and awareness that love is the ultimate. (Have written this to him.)

1 September

Went to see Fr M.I. had a most rewarding time, he said as I left, "We are very close, very close," it is true, I felt this at the very beginning, and so it has grown. I told him of my eye trouble, I had not mentioned it before, he said I should have, he used his ministry upon me, very gently. I was aware, it took a little time and a line came to me which repeated itself over and over again. "Lord, I believe, help thou my unbelief." I felt a sharp piercing sensation, at the back of the left eye, it stopped later, but it still feels a little touchy.

17 November

Yesterday's visit was indeed remarkable, not only for the words received before I saw him "Love's contemplation of suffering" which were so right and applicable to him, but the complete opening up of himself…due no doubt to the shock of something happening to him entirely unforeseen. This, and all said between us, must remain in complete confidence, so I shall record nothing here, how very blessed I am to be used in this way, as I go forth, I think on a completely different level with him and now I must write…there is deep peace and the ever-deepening awareness of the growth of love through Our Lord.

30 November

During intercession, prayer to the Holy Mother for Fr M.I., the word 'Poverty' again made itself known to me…there came a clear picture of the Priest at the altar and his offering of Our Lord to the people…the words also returned at this point "Love's contemplation of suffering" as Our Lord contemplates the suffering of his servant so the servant must contemplate the suffering of those whom the Lord loves…"And he went among men and healed them." The Lord was born into poverty…and to share fully in his suffering this too must be shared, known and experienced…to work and to heal amongst it?

11 December

Fr M.I. telephoned and all is indeed well, he said, "a beautiful letter and exactly right," we talked about it. Then quite unreservedly. Prayer today, a return of the words "Love's contemplation of suffering"…a descent into darkness!

20 December

When my director telephoned in an answer to my letter, one line he said registered with me, "one loses one's identity." My immediate thought was 'you have not chosen me, I have chosen you', a priest never loses his identity in the sight of God. This morning somebody I know who does voluntary work at St Botolph's Aldgate sent me a Christmas card, the front was a real photograph of a Priest at the altar, Midnight Mass…it was absolutely identical with my vision in the prayer of X! Deo gratias.

1982

6 January

Saw my director two days ago, much was talked about, regarding himself also and the future! Do have reservations on some points…but he has to be shown himself, and I pray this will be so…I do feel he is afraid of a different step…and I do understand this, at the same time I think it is necessary – whatever form it may take. I had a bad 24 hours over one point, but now see it was a hurt pride, so I am thankful to have realised it, tranquillity has returned! Rest in the darkness and wait.

12 January

Prayer within the darkness, much is received in this regarding my director! My own uncertainty has passed – I can only say what I received. This came and was intensified over a long period…as the centre is learning the immersion of itself in darkness, it is aware of change…there flows from it a constant intercessory prayer for all whom it knows, loves and has constant contact with, leading to the prayer for mankind in its pain and longing (realised or not) for God…equally there flows into it love, there is new depth, yet another level to which it gives itself freely and unreservedly…it is empty, yet full. Silence within the silence, silence within the living of everyday life, a deep pool, untroubled and undisturbed.

2 March

I was in the Lady Chapel and could just see the Reserved Sacrament upon the High Altar between the brick pillars, my being was riveted upon it. The Priesthood, in its truest sense, came to mind, 'Heal the sores of Lazarus', perhaps this is the answer to Fr M.I. and what I have been shown…it would be a far cry from ministering in Chelsea to a slum area, I don't know, yet it came clearly to me…I can only pass it on.

8 March

Had a long and interesting discussion with my director on many issues, it is good to be able to talk so freely…much is emerging about himself and his future, during prayer, I was drawn to great depth praying that God will show him the way…over and over came the line for him 'The poverty of Christ is the wealth of the Father' I told him before I left him waiting upon God, thoughts did come regarding my director, his unknown generosity in certain quarters…his utter loneliness.

25 April

I wrote the following for my director's 55th birthday.

The Priest

Before the altar of God,
I am ever reminded of the call to follow him…
I am chosen…
My yoke is upon me.
I have been led through impenetrable darkness,
Yet aware of ineffable light.
Endured blindness where nothing is 'seen',
Yet is there 'known',
The act of consecration, he is held within my hand,
It matters nothing, whether there be darkness or light within my span.
I am his chosen one,
He is my beloved Lord.

10 May

I went to see Director! I laughed inwardly when he referred to "Union with God: The Teaching of St. John of The Cross," sent him by DT. "It is quite good and he does have a good brain," he said. I do see this as a good opening that they be drawn together, the problem with the kind of people they both are…and very different…they will both find it very difficult to open to each other…hopefully it will come in time, I think they have much to offer if only they will recognise it.

11 May

My director did say yesterday of himself, that the medical side is receding as the priest comes more and more to the forefront of his awareness. I continue to pray that he be shown his road.

12 May

My director also said regarding DT, "You should not leave him, he is part of your spiritual life…although you must not treat him the same as your sons."

I said in reply, "I do not look upon myself as his mother."

(At Burnham Abbey) In the chapel, I found myself and found is the operative word…in deepest prayer regarding my director, perhaps it is because I know how deeply he loves this place, that strong and insistent thoughts that it is here, perhaps within their context of the Mass, that he will come to know his road...there are other thoughts also that I shall not commit here, but write to him. I felt so spiritually attuned to him I cannot ignore it.

23 May

Mass...aridity...but later, the altar at Burnham Abbey was within me...the priest kneeling – and over all, the Dove hovered...my prayer continues for him that his way becomes clear to him. I found this on a deep level, and it remains in my conscious mind.

25 May

I opened the Bible at random and read Hebrews chapters 6 and 7...which is about the priesthood of Christ and of Melchizedek! I do not think this is a coincidence, but entirely relevant to what I have been receiving from my director (Have written to him as I think he should know this.)

27 May

Director telephoned for prayer regarding certain issues.

7 July

Visited director...I told him I was afraid to proceed into this deeper arid state...that equally I knew I must. He said, "There is nothing to be afraid of," in that sense 'no', it probably is the ever-deepening pain I sense it will bring. He needs a professional ear, so I hope my suggestion will bear fruit.

8 July

The last 20 minutes was spent in prayer as we normally do, almost immediately the centre was carried deep into darkness and to the edge of the deeper aridity...it clearly 'heard' the voice "This is truth...enter in..." even as it hesitated it took two steps and was over the edge...there followed the most harrowing and excruciating pain of Spirit...it felt completely stripped of all that covered it...disguised it...that it was held naked of any sham it possessed, and exposed to the eye of discernment and of truth…there was coldness…finally the director said, "Amen."

"I received from you wave upon wave of pain,"

All I could say was, "Yes."

He said, "You will come through, I think it is the same as I experienced before I wrote my last book."

24 September

Saw my director two days ago…I never cease to be amazed at the rapport between us…during the silent prayer there was only love…it ran as a silver stream, we agreed that if either of us were ill, or known to be dying, that the other would be notified and come, he said, "There are not many I would say this to." I am at Hemingford Grey. I did ask him when I last saw him if he thought my writing had finished, he said, "It could be"…now I am here I wonder…

The last address on the fruits of silence, strangely enough, was on peace…at one point regarding himself (M.I.) he said, "I am shy, vulnerable and totally inadequate." I was very close to tears…why was this? I know him, he may think himself as inadequate, I know what he means, it is Christ in him, as any good any of us do is Christ within us…I have learnt a great deal in this retreat. I do have reservations about learning that he is to be the priest in charge of the parish where he is an assistant priest (Holy Trinity, Prince Consort Road). I have said nothing, time will tell…I still believe he must experience true poverty…he will not experience it where he is, although he will experience poverty of mind and spirit there, perhaps that is it! Yet the words return, "Heal the sores of Lazarus" for this moment, I shall keep silence. De Caussade and the practice of the present moment…to be where we are…use each moment as it is given.

(On the 3 September 1983, Ivy writes as follows: At Mass this morning, I think I realised fully for the first time the part of the Holy Mother, the same probably applies to prayers for my director (M.I.) The sudden realisation of why 'poverty' was repeatedly within me regarding (them). I mistook this for a long time, my (prejudice) was in the way here, thinking (they were) being called to experience material poverty…not so…it is the poverty of loss…love and all stemming from this most important of all childhood expectations…deprivation…The poverty of Spirit.)

16 October

Saw the director two days ago, much was talked about, it is so good how our relationship is deepening, I learnt that I am one of the two 'ears' he uses, and who the other one is. I have seen her at retreats and felt very drawn to her, he told me some of her background and life...there has been much suffering in it, yet nothing to do with poverty, but the reverse. I don't suppose I will ever meet her or know her!

5 December

To the director's church, most beautiful,

Architecture I found it all very uplifting and, something else that is getting less in many places...i.e. reverence. The first Sunday of the month is choral Mattins and Holy Communion, so in future when I go I shall make it on the first Sunday. The old prayer book all came back to me and it was most refreshing during the actual communion. I was very aware of the Priest at the altar...the presence of the Dove was very clear to me, not only at the altar but within the man...words were clearly given "He is beloved of God"...and these remain. There is most definitely a spiritual affinity, I pray to God with thanksgiving.

1983

15 January

The words of my director returned to me unbidden, "I am a humble man"...I know if he ever reads this he will understand, and anyone who reads this too...humility in oneself is not recognised as a grace by oneself.

30 January

Director telephoned tonight regarding Christopher, also the director and friend have now met...he says it all went very well...deep level...'I think he trusts me'! Deo gratias...

2 March

Yesterday, I went to my director's, much talked about...a couple of remarks regarding Mirfield on one hand and J on the other, surprised me by their tartness…one lives and learns…during silent prayer together this time, my inner thoughts were not stilled…perhaps a rest is indicated! So much concerning other people has come from my visit to Mirfield!

4 May

Visited the director last week…much was talked about…during prayer at the end…the river of love with the twin rocks of faith and hope…the rocks crumbled into pieces and were absorbed within the water…all is one within love…Director said he thought I should not go to communities again, unless for a definite reason…this is how I felt any way…they have served their purpose…Spiritually I am empty…

7 May

I was talking to my director about death. It holds no fears for him…he sees the transition for himself and for me as being easy, although one cannot foresee the manner of one's death regarding pain, etc. Putting life and faith aside, the word that is most bearable to me is not from life to death but from life to the reality of hope fulfilled. The death of loved ones is probably much harder to come to terms with, and the love/hate relationships of people we are bound to by blood ties.

21 June

To Director…there was much shared, after our prayer time together, which was shorter than usual because so much talking was got through, he said, "Your spiritual progress is incredible to me and slowly coming towards sanctification"…I write this but am certainly not repeating it to even my closest friend…I do not 'feel' anything regarding this, it really is as though I am looking at somebody apart from myself. I do accept, however, whatever God shows to me, without questioning the whys and wherefores…there is a depth within my very core that is unexplainable, it just is. I have spoken to my director about my recognition of the 'aged face of beauty' shown to me as Mother Julian. He does agree and says that he himself is very close to her as well. The more we go on together, the more I realise how right it was that I was led to him that whatever one believes is impossible, is possible with faith.

O incredible love that leads me on beyond the horizon of earthly sight,
The will is done,
The soul, led here and there, drifting from its true course, is stilled at last
The core immediately fixed upon thee,
Accepts thy invitation.
To drink deeply from the preferred cup.
Carried forth on the wings of the Dove…it soars.

26 June

During Mass this morning, thoughts came upon what I had mentioned briefly to my director regarding the son at the altar (Priest). I know how many years it took for my director to forgive his parents for what they had done to him…but specific thoughts come today for his mother and himself. She has been dead for many years, there came to me unbidden, knowledge of love freed from all earthly ills, she knew now as we cannot know, the strength/power of the call of the Father upon her son…the perception of the whole that she is now given shows it was no accident of birth that she delivered/bore him, only that the Father's will has been fulfilled. What she was never aware of in this world has been clearly shown her in the hereafter the love she never knew, or indeed, was incapable of giving, flows now in thanksgiving, entering this world as all purified love enters this world, strengthening wherever it flows, so at this late hour her son receives from his mother a benediction…Deo gratias.

30 June

The director rang me regarding my letter to him, concerning what I was shown above (26 June). He said, "It is absolutely authentic, thank you so much, I am very grateful."

31 August

Yesterday at the director's, a great deal was talked about, I took the Church Times with me so he could read the notice of his latest book 'Spirit of Counsel'. He gave me a copy and said he would like me to say what I think about it. (I am going to have to begin charging!). There is a great rapport between us, "The Holy Spirit." I received the laying on of hands and the anointing. This was at my request and to do with what lies ahead before my friend and myself…it was extremely moving. There came a clear 'picture' of a friend before the Calvary (at Mirfield) and later came the words 'to release the imprisoned soul. I showed M.I. what had been clarified regarding the infant weeping in the womb, I wanted his assurance that it was correct. He says that what we are and what we shall become is formed within the womb! Does this make allowances for upbringing, environment, etc.? Some little time later, having read the chapter in his book that he says is the most important, the identity crisis. I see very clearly how to be marked in the womb applies so relevantly to him, I have written to him on this matter.

10 September

The following from M.I. book 'Spirit of Counsel' p. 135

'It must be said that some of the most remarkable people, it has been my privilege to know them, have come from such appalling backgrounds that psychological and sociological theory would have condemned them summarily to delinquency and irreversible emotional breakdown. Instead, you have shown me the way of love and sanctity.'

I think this is one of the best books he has written, although I must agree with Neville Ward, who wrote of it in the Church Times, I do find the constant biblical references very irritating, it is not for everybody, of course, nothing ever is, it also shows a great deal about himself – one knows him well enough. There is much I could write – but will not.

6 December

My director took what I had put to him, regarding a friend very calmly, as I thought he would. I explained a little to him, I thought it unfair not to. He finally said, "How you must love him." There is no answer to that!

24 December

I telephoned my director as he has been in and out of my thoughts for 2–3 days for no specific reason. He said he had been in a period of psychic darkness which was just beginning to lift. How strange this is (yet, of course, not strange at all!)

1984

30 January

I went to see the director, had a very interesting talk, spiritually he suggests I wait. He said the first part of my work was finished. Now, I wait and see what is to be…it is what I have already written, but I did ask him if I should do more now on a practical level i.e. Samaritans, P.C.C., visiting etc, but he advised against it, so I shall take his advice. We did talk about our inner selves but I have already clarified my thoughts on this and will probably write.

7 April

Went to see the director, much talked about, all very constructive for me. I learn more and more regarding his inner thoughts. Man's Gethsemane, as I understand it, is Christ's Gethsemane also, they are one and the same. I learn more and more how fragile the strongest people are. We were talking (M.I.) about the books he has written, I said to him, "Each one comes nearer and nearer to love? What more can one ask?"

He replied, "What more indeed." Within our prayer together, the inner eye was drawn to the place of desolation, but as the pain assailed the centre, it bore it and passed it to our Blessed Lord. This then is what has been given, we bear nothing in our own strength. I cannot say that the pain lessened, it still had to be borne, but it was not borne alone. I opened my eyes before he opened his, I thought (bearing in mind what he has said) how vulnerable he was.

4 June

My time with my director this afternoon was so rewarding, so much shared, he has had an operation for a detached retina, and the sight is slowly returning to normal, it takes time. When I told him of my meeting with the children at Ron's grave, he referred to it as an encounter. "That," he said, "is how it will be in heaven, there is no doubt that Ron was very near at that time." I did realise afterwards that the 'encounter' as he called it, was a healing. We talked together in great depth and it is good. "Ron will be waiting for you," he said, "and you will walk together." He really is a very perceptive man, and as he admitted, a lonely one also, but he has his work, healing…retreats…writing…a priest. He read me a poem 'The black boy', 'Black skin but my soul is white' I am so moved by much that he says to me, our shared prayer as far as I was concerned, was for him.

29 September

Yesterday, I went to see the director, more and more he is talking about himself, this is so good, and I believe it is necessary for him, I feel much sadness at some of the things he says, so much loneliness, no close relatives at all, much I could write, but it would not be wise to do so. One should feel no surprise at the fears and thoughts of others, it is just that when one hears them voiced from a person like him, an author, counsellor, healer, doctor and priest, one tends to forget, to put aside their own humanity and ability to suffer pain, as though they were immune, they are far from immune, their own need is probably greater than those they help. My own daily prayer of "Use me, Lord" is certainly heard and answered.

1986

4 September

Had a very good talk with my director today. He was not too well, having broken his collarbone, plus a nasty tooth abscess. After prayer at the end, I asked him if he had received the laying on of hands, he said he had not, there was nobody he felt able to ask or wished to ask…I had been thinking since he phoned me last week that he needed it and he should have it…and I must admit that the thought had entered my mind, but I had dismissed it, nevertheless, it materialised, for he asked me if I would do it for him, that there was nobody he would sooner have. I did hesitate momentarily, but I did do it. I prayed silently that he would be so infused with the power of God's love that evil would flee before it I then spoke these words, "Lord, receive Martin, thy child." All was so well and will be so well. As he had said earlier, "We have an affinity." Within prayer, the inner eye returned to the spiritual heart of Our Lord.

12 September

Have just learnt that my director is to go into hospital tomorrow for an operation on his collarbone/shoulder.

20 September

Went to see my director in hospital yesterday. I thought immediately about how vulnerable he was. We talked about his situation, especially his future work, and when he leaves hospital, I have written suggesting what could be an initial help. One interesting thing my director told me, that he began his medical career in 1953 at Langthorne Hospital. It was then and is now a geriatric hospital, but it is the same Langthorne mentioned in my autobiography that used to be the workhouse and in which my mother left me when I was seven years old.

12 November

Saw the director yesterday, not very satisfactory from my point of view, but that was probably my fault. I saw something that upset me on my way to him, so was not in a suitable frame of mind. I was not able to shake this off, our shared prayer time at the end was empty. He said afterwards, "That was a deeply shared meditation? No comment?" There are various pinpricks lately that I have not found easy, all is not always sweetness and light! Fortunately, the effects do not last long.

7 December

Something very important has happened between the director and me. There is much future work here, he said, I had changed, become sterner, but that it was good as it denoted a growth in inner strength. I was not aware of this myself but the fact remains that without inner strength, one cannot help others to the same degree. Probably this has happened through the emotional pain I have suffered since Ron's death (on 3 May). Hopefully, one emerges stronger from this. Sternness etc, however, must always be tempered with love and compassion, sternness on its own would be of no avail. (My director) says also he is sure that writing will start up again, he is probably right because I stopped it…it was not stopped for me.

1987

5 February

Had a very good and constructive talk yesterday with the director, it is true that one is not able to see oneself in complete truth, or as other people see us, but some of the things he says to me about myself? I am not able to see myself in them. I am sure this is how it should be, and I listen, then let it go. I talked to him about 'The still waters of love'. It is thirteen years since this was received at West Mailing. Time, of course, means nothing to God, and his purposes will be worked out for however long it takes. There is so much to be learnt from this, not least patience, to wait…forever if need be, upon God, eventually, it will be so.

24 February

I have finished reading M.I. book 'Gethsemane, the transfiguring love'. I think it is one of the best books he has written, although at times I feel it is no book for a depressive to read, but the last two chapters redeem all that. As Mother Julian of Norwich said, 'Love is my meaning' and it is and shall be love that shall redeem all. I doubt there are many people that can express themselves in such a definitive way upon the subject of Christ's Passion and the descent into hell but it is indeed a revelation. The end of us, as he says, is the beginning of us, and if one has experienced one's own Gethsemane and emerged into the true light that has its being in the travail of darkness, it is simplicity. Theological arguments and all they entail, intellectual reasoning etc, all these things are nothing in the light of simple truth enclosed in love I found his comments on St John of the Cross interesting, some people evidently seeing him as a depressive, even so, even if he was, look what has come from this! Opposite to this, of course, one could point to Mother Julian of Norwich, whose whole totality was the exposition of love, i.e. Divine Love, we are each as God made us, and it behoves us to use our individual gifts for good in his name. I do understand now more fully the meaning of celibacy, perhaps in its truest sense, not given to many people.

30 July

Today I saw my director, sharing…good and fruitful. Just before I left he said, "Shall I give you the laying on of hands?" This was totally unexpected, no reason was given, and I did not ask. Next Sunday, if it is not pouring with rain, I shall go to his church. I should make more effort to go on a regular basis, but it is quite a long way, and a lot of walking too, it is something I should do, we share so much spiritually, and as for me, it is important to receive from him. Quite obviously, it is something he would like as well.

3 August

Today to the director's church. I realised how he was ageing. I don't notice it so much when I see him at his home, he is sitting down, but this morning, he looks much older than his 60 years. His address, as always, was excellent, the Holy Spirit, the fruits of the Spirit and to a lesser degree, the gifts of the Spirit. Today was choral Eucharist, so Communion was taken before the high altar. It is a beautiful church. The service is BCP. I know he would like to change this, but it is difficult. I still felt as I did before, a certain amount of stiffness and coldness from the congregation, but it is always difficult when in a church that is not one's regular place of worship, and I am sure that this should not be. It was good nevertheless to be there and receive from him, my prayer is for him. One of the fruits of the Spirit listed by M.I. was self-control, but in a different context to how I had understood it, "to listen without interruption, not to break in with one's own thoughts etc before the person had finished speaking" and how many people had asked him, "Do I know God?" His answer is "When you bear the fruits of the Spirit, i.e. love, peace and joy, then you know God."

1988

23 February

Went to see the director. He referred to what I had sent him as very impressive'. I just said to him that I accept it and do not question it (the writings I mean) because this is the only way I can deal with it. Jeffrey said not long ago that I should have it published now. He was thinking only of the monetary gain, for my benefit now, but it is not to be so. This is nothing to do with my earthly gain and it is for D.B.T. and M.I. to do after my death. Also, it is still being received by me, it is not finished, and at what point do I say "this is the end." It is difficult, I suppose, for those who do not think this way, to understand. M.I. gave me his latest book today, "The pearl of great price, a journey to the Kingdom."

11 July

Last Friday, I visited M.I. I wanted to discuss with him the break from spiritual writing that I felt I needed, although the last two weeks are yet to be written to complete the seven veils of love, and which I shall do. I shall not record here what he said, as it is of a deeply personal nature, except to say that he does not see himself as my spiritual director (I must be guided completely by the Holy Spirit). He has said this before, but nevertheless, I have always regarded him as my director. This time he made it very clear indeed that the basis of my visits to him is friendship alone. I do not want to be understood here or thought to have 'false humility', but I find this very difficult. It is, I suppose, because of who he is, his work, the place he holds in life, etc. This does not prevent me 'seeing clearly' however, and this is I suppose what he realises too, so I accept this as a great privilege and will in our future contact be open both to receive and give fully.

16 November

I saw M.I. today, at one point I was very moved by the look on his face as he spoke of a certain friend who has been dead seven and a half years.
(This friend was Fr Geoffrey Curtis C.R.)

30 November

This morning I received confirmation of a retreat to be conducted next August by M.I. His retreats are booked up so quickly, it is unbelievable, so I am very happy to have 'got in'. I phoned him to tell him, knowing that he too would be happy at this, as indeed he was. He asked how I was and I said, "Very well apart from toothache and a swollen face." His concern always surprises me, he gave me a little lecture (in the nicest possible way) making me promise to make a dental appointment and to let him know. I daren't do otherwise, but have to wait eight days, so I hope it gets no worse before then. I suppose my reaction to him is within me. For one thing, I am not used to being cared for, and I find it difficult to accept our friendship because of who he is, although it is getting easier all the time. I have so much to be thankful for!

15 December

M.I. telephoned last night to see how I was. I am very grateful for his concern. He has been asked to a parishioner's for Christmas dinner, after which he will have a few days away, as he said, "Christmas is not a good time for me, you will have your family all around you." I know what loneliness is and it can affect the most well-adjusted people. I have never experienced his kind of loneliness, where there is no family at all, or friends that are close enough to share with, and I feel helpless because there is nothing I can do to ease the situation.

1989

3 April

M.I. has given me his latest book, 'The Quest for Wholeness'. It is much more autobiographical and I shall enjoy that. Our time together was good, he is very pleased with the gift I gave him and said, "I shall treasure it" referring to it, or should I say myself, as "so like Julian of Norwich." I have to see the funny side of this, it is the only way I can cope.

15 June

Letter from M.I. in answer to writing on 'self-esteem', was very good. What he is saying is 'holy indifference'. Which is given a great deal as one journey the 'road', not always though, for some people never lose their absorption with self, and until this is achieved, progress at any depth will not be made!

12 July

A friend told me on the phone this morning that M.I. has been in hospital with a broken toe, I am due to see him on the 27th, so hope all is well by then.

24 July

Was able to contact M.I. today at the hospital, but he should be home by Thursday 27, when I shall see him, it was his ankle he has broken – not his toe.

28 July, Yesterday, I went to the director. I am getting less and less inclined to make the journey, but I must go for as long as I am able, M looked quite well considering all things, he does have difficulty walking, as one would expect. Much was discussed, relaxed and uninhibited. Within our prayer together, the inner eye was drawn again to the 'ground of love' and…the words immediately within me "Have you still not learnt the lesson of love?" I talked to M about this and he too was at a loss, except to say "It will be shown." (When) M said the "Amen" I had difficulty coming out of this, as I know he saw, although he did not know the reason and I did not tell him. He was looking at me as I opened my eyes, with that very direct look that is typical of him. The very first time I saw him, August 1976, among other things, he asked me how old I was, now after 13 years, I reminded him and asked if he could remember what he meant. "Yes," he said, "What I meant was that you were not too old to fulfil your potential."

25 August

Today, I go into retreat at St Katharine's, it would be an understatement to say "I am looking forward to it."(After some detailed description of the addresses, Ivy writes) I do find his many references nonliteral/rather irritating also to his mother's mental state, which again would have been better left unsaid. It detracts from her wholeness, she has been dead for many years and will have grown out of all knowledge. It is not how she was here that is important, but how she is now. The question must be asked, "Why?" His own pain has obviously not yet gone.

2 October

Today, I visited M.I. as always it was so good. I do learn many things that are helpful to me, bearing in mind he is also a doctor. He said to me, "Yours is a ministry of love, isn't it?" I had never thought this, I had never put a name to it, but it did give me a tremendous spiritual lift to hear him say it. We talked so much out, I shall go to his church 'Holy Trinity' on Advent Sunday! He is looking so much better than when I saw him at St Katharine's and walking much better also, after his broken ankle.

1990

18 January

This morning to see M.I. We talked a great deal through and I was most grateful for his advice on certain matters. I was agreeably surprised at his thoughts on my moving to Lincolnshire. He is all for it, he asked if I would still be able to see him. I replied it depends on my getting out. He could always come and stay with me if he ever wanted to. I really cannot see myself travelling from Lincolnshire for an hour but if I could overnight with D or anyone else in the London area, then I would make a point of seeing him. After our prayer time together, I said to him, "It really doesn't matter if I do not see you again, does it?" and he agreed. Spiritual friendships do not necessarily require physical presence, although this does not mean that it is not always so good to meet, because it is this sort of closeness together which always includes God, it can easier bear such partings and we both understood this. Much of what he said on another matter, I am not going to write. I should have a very large head, complete with a halo and wings to boot. He has given me his latest book "Creation, the consummation of the world." as he said, "It is different." One other thing I write about is that others may be helped. I told him of my breakdown with Jeffrey on Christmas Eve.

We were driving to Doddinghurst and various things were being talked about, when suddenly and without warning, I began to cry. It went on and on, when we reached his home I said, "You must back out and drive around. I can't go in." So he did and very gradually it subsided. Looking back, I realised that it was not specifically what was being spoken of, which was Neil, but an accumulation of what has been happening over the last five and a half years. There had never been an outlet, one must always be strong for others etc.

M.I. said, "It is a good thing it happened, you had to confront your own weakness. I have had to do the same." The words "you had to confront your own weakness" are the operative words, they have taught me a great deal and apply to us all, of own strength we can do nothing, what we are able to do is from God, who is our strength, but when this happens personally, two things happen, one is to 'see' how weak one is, and fallible, and the other is to stand up straight and carry on. My thanks to M.I.

8 February

See the first two chapters, which I did not absorb very easily. The last chapter called 'The consummation of all things' I liked very much, quote "What we are in process of achieving in this mortal life of ours at the present time is the fashioning of a spiritual body that will be our form when we have left the physical one behind us at the moment of death, it returns to the earth from whose elements it was composed, but the immaterial mind/soul complex goes forth into the mental/psychic/spiritual realm clothed in a spiritual body whose elements are the thoughts and attitudes we manifested while we were engaged in earthly activity." This really does hold deep meaning for me. Have looked up Matthew 22, 1–14, especially 11–14 that was quoted and now understood.

13 March

Yesterday to M.I., it was a glorious spring day, today is quite the reverse! Our time together was so good, so much shared, we were talking of my prospective move to Spalding, when he quite suddenly referred to the 'Song of Songs', he fetched a bible and read aloud from chapter 8, he did not quote the first few lines, but began "Place me like a seal over your heart, like a seal on your arm: for love is as strong as death, its jealousy unyielding as the grave, it burns like a blazing fire, like a mighty flame, many waters cannot quench love, rivers cannot wash it away." At this point he stopped, the pieces he emphasised are those I have underlined, I was, and am deeply touched by this, and I would refer to the last two lines of the above on daffodils (This poem above this entry finishes with the two lines "So much in the perceiving, Do you give to me."). When talking of marriage (the fact that he is not married), one thing led to another, as it quite often does, and with two different couples I had in mind, I said to him, "It is said that within marriage one loves and is loved," and perhaps this is how it is in some friendships, with regard to myself, I think it is I who is loved more deeply than I am able to love, I don't know, because one never 'sees' oneself in the way we are seen. When I said, "You are a very gifted man."

He answered, "Yes, I am," which at that point made me want to laugh, but he added some seconds later, "and a very lonely one as well." All in all, I have so very much to be thankful for, not the least of having such a friendship. Within our shared prayer, there came the awareness of the present moment (de Caussade), and in that moment came the knowledge of love, that moment became the following moment, and so on, so that the initial pinpoint that was recognised as love expanded accordingly, then, it meant that one other person in the room, and the things in that room that spoke clearly of that person, the plant in flower, a beloved photograph, the pictures on the wall that must have individual meaning to their owner, the icons, crosses, religious objects, books, the feeling of the solidity of the furniture, especially the armchair where so many people sit, at ease, or not, as the case may be, this is a room that has held so many confidences, perhaps a book should be written called 'The Room'.

(This meeting is pivotal. Ivy is to leave London soon to live in Lincolnshire near her youngest son, Jeffrey. As is so often the case when a relationship ceases to be expressed in a particular way, in this case, regular meeting and prayer, those in the relationship articulate more clearly than is usually what they mean to each other. So it is in this case.).

30 April

I shall see M.I. later this morning, it is his 63rd birthday and the anniversary of the death of his friend, Fr Geoffrey Curtiss C.R. My time spent with him was very rewarding indeed. He was leaving in the early afternoon to conduct a retreat at Pleshey. There is so much shared now. I told him of (my experience), a spiritual communion I felt called to make last week and the difference of not receiving in the mouth but absorbed straight into the heart. He said this was wonderful and held important meaning. I asked him what this was, he said, "It's between you and Jesus."

3 July

I saw M.I. This proved as always very fruitful. I did have a painful backache, I believe, due to lifting a piece of lead that was in the shed. His first comment was "You look wan." We discussed many issues, which was a great help to me, he also spoke of my writing, but I really feel I can take no credit for this. As I have said before, I am aware of being used, I am open to receiving, and the rest is of God.

11 August

When I last saw M.I. he spoke of the writing and thought it may be approaching its zenith. Whether what has been written recently is the zenith, I do not know, it could well be, I have given some thought as to what may happen when/if I move, I have to leave that and wait and see, I have no way of knowing, I am sure it will not disappear altogether…There will be new happenings, new people, descriptive writing, for it will all be completely different and I am ready to meet this. As far as all that has been written goes, all has been a learning process.

13 November

Yesterday to M.I. There is nothing I can write here, it is too personal. I am most unhappy, experienced a very restless night. Was not prepared for such an adverse reaction to my moving, will go to his church on Advent Sunday. He has given me his latest book – the 16th – 'A light on the path – an exploration of integrity through the Psalms.'

16 November

Through prayer, etc., I am now back on an even keel. I am amazed at what looks like a deep insensitivity on my part, a failure to see deeply enough another's pain and bereftness. Another lesson learned. I have written to M.

21 November

Received a letter from M this morning. It is a good letter, obviously, he had time to get things into perspective. I know that I caught him unaware when I said, "My house is sold, I shall be moving soon." Originally it was to be in the spring of 91. It all first escalated very swiftly, however, as he has written, "we shall keep in close contact by the letter." My thoughts have turned to the book written by Rose Macaulay, 'Letters to a friend'. It is not beyond the bounds of possibility that this could happen between M and myself. The more I ponder on this, the more possible it seems. He writes also, "It will be good to feed you with the Body and Blood of Our Lord Jesus Christ on Advent Sunday – a fitting zenith of our time together in London." All in all, much good has come from it all, all will carry on at a different level. Deo gratias.

3 December

Yesterday was Advent Sunday and I went, as promised to M.I.'s church, Holy Trinity, Prince Consort Road S.W. 7. This is a tiring journey for me, which is why I have not made it very often, as I have written before, the interior belies the exterior, it was built 1901–6, designed by the Victorian architect George Bodley, the very high pulpit reminds me of those in Italy, I remember the one in Amalfi, especially, as that is where I first saw the Pieta, this has remained clearly within. The high altar and reredos at Holy Trinity are so beautiful, I arrived early and sat for some time looking at it and trying to imprint it in my memory, as this was to be the last time I shall see it. (Ivy moved to Holbeach in Lincolnshire on 25 January 1991) M.I. looked physically frail, whether there are spinal problems, I don't know, it seems so to look at him. There are no servers, and at some point during the service, he almost fell as he went up and down the steps to the credence table, physically he is an old 63 years, close to, however, he looks quite well and his voice is as clear as ever, I felt deep unhappiness about him and the future of his church should it be closed, as he himself said, "People come from all over to hear him preach," that is what keeps the church open, but may not be allowed by the bishop for too much longer. Will he see this as a further redundancy, a further (as he sees it) rejection? I have no idea what the music was before the service, but loved it! His address was good, stressing the 'value of the present moment', and penitence, of course during the Advent season. "The Zenith," as he wrote in his letter, was to be the "feeding of the Body and Blood of Our Lord Jesus Christ" and this is what it was, the zenith, as he placed the Host in my hands, he put his index finger over it while he said the words, "Receive the Body of Our Lord Jesus Christ that was given for you and feed on him in your heart by faith with thanksgiving." By doing this. I was unable to put it into my mouth until he had finished speaking. As I write this the following morning, this remains clearly within, the inner eye dwells upon it continuously, this will be my strength and courage in whatsoever lies ahead, I cannot say what my feelings, which is probably a totally inappropriate word, were, quiet I think, calm, meditative, no great splurge of emotion, nothing like that at all, just peace. After that, since I saw him very briefly, at the back. I smiled and so did he, I said, taking his hand, "goodbye"…a chapter has ended, may God be with him. Referring back to the placing of his finger on the Host which was lying in my hand, this it is that 'sets the seal' Song of Songs 8, 6 etc…I had thought later, on what a beautiful thing a true spiritual friendship can be, two people and Our Lord, he is who brought them together, who gave it to them and nurtured it, who taught them the meaning of love that has its roots in him, with love comes truth and fidelity. (*Of course, it was not goodbye. They continued to speak on the telephone and write to each other.*)

1991

9 January

Amid all the trauma of moving, prayer continues within, since I went to M.I.'s church on Advent Sunday, the receiving from him and the manner in which he emphasised this by placing his finger on the Host in my cupped hands, has remained with me. I understood the significance at the time and knew that the recalling of it would prove a strength and a comfort to me, and so it is.

3 March

I am receiving letters from M.I. almost by return of those I write, they are lovely letters, he is much in my prayers.

8 May

Received a letter from M.I. I still seem to be slow at recognising what this friendship means to him, I pray for him.

1992

14 February

I have replied to M.I. letter and kept a copy of what I have written so there can be no misunderstanding of what has or has not been written...I would like to say that all the pieces I have written over the years are in fact from prayer, either for myself or as I have seen the needs of others. Words come inwardly, I just write them down.

20 February

Yesterday, I received a reply from M.I. He has, in fact, admitted he was wrong, so that has been aired, leave it. At least, it was brought to a head and he has got it out of his system. One really does not know what lies within others, even those we are closest to.

30 April

M.I.'s 51st birthday. I had written that I would be with him in prayer as he conducted the Mass at 11.45 am today, This I have done, my prayer was deep, not only for his priesthood but for his human need and this is great. I thought when it came to the consecration and the elevation of the Host that I would be able to make a spiritual communion, that was my intention, but I was unable to do it. It is difficult to explain, one would think it would just be done, but not so…It may be that he was not in church today, he may have been away conducting a retreat, it is of no consequence, and wherever he was he was held before Our Lord.

16 June

Received an answer from M.I. this morning, advising me to try and find my half-sister, Kathleen, "maybe she seeks your help either here or on the other side of life" etc. I am quite grateful for all he has written. I am writing first to the missing person's bureau of the Salvation Army. Kathleen joined the A.T.S. in 1941, so there may be a lead there. I do know that if it is God's will that we meet, then it will be if, however, she is dead and perhaps the reason why my mother's presence is so clear and so definite to me, then spiritually much shall be given.

(In the event, Ivy never managed to trace Kathleen.)

16 July

Following upon M.I.'s very wise advice to pray for my father and sister, has opened up very much within me and it is, I believe, freeing me of any inhibitions about them that I wasn't aware that I had. My father is not Kathleen's father, so from that point of view, she is excluded from any understanding I may be given regarding him.

30 July

(A local priest) made an interesting comment when he realised that I knew M.I. "I went to one of his Priests' retreats and sat next to him during meal times, he was silent, I felt as though he was almost ethereal in an ever descending vale and that I was being drawn down with him." How revealing this is. Later, I realised that all was well with me, I seemed to have descended briefly into the darkness, and the printed words in the (new) book written by M.I. seemed to enmesh me. It lasted about 36 hours, enough to affect me but am now returned to my usual habitat. This can only be an infinitesimal part of what M.I. experiences, all I can do is to continue to hold him in the light that is Christ.

4 August

Have been gradually reading through the book of Job. I know it is one of M.I.'s favourite books. Chapter 28, I attune to, what is wisdom, what is understanding? Right in the last verse (28) "The fear of the Lord, that is wisdom and to shun evil is understanding."

17 September

Returned this afternoon from London saw M.I. I was totally unprepared for what he was going to ask of me, to be his ear and support in his times of deep depression, this is to be by phone. I thought afterwards it is like being a Samaritan again – a listening car – his mainstay and support that he has relied on for a long time has died. He has asked if I can take her place. I do count this a privilege and hope I can fulfil it successfully, he used to ring her at 10.30 pm each night, and sometimes in the early hours. 10.30 pm will not be a problem, the early hours I am not so sure about. I gave this much thought over the following 24 hours, wondering how I can combat these severe depressions and the knowledge of evil given to him and without which he says he would be unable to write his books. I awoke last Thursday morning, 16 September, about 6.30 am wide-awake, my thoughts reverted to him and I began to pray. Somewhere along the line, I became aware of the words given to me before I left for London, these are, of course, the antidote, "Blessed is he who comes in the name of the Lord." This really is incredible, that I should receive them before I knew how they were going to be used. Thanksgiving.

21 September

St Matthew's Day and the 17th anniversary of M.I.'s ordination. I prayed for him, especially that he may learn to trust any with whom he believes he has a deep friendship (his words) The time is drawing near when I shall see him again, it is one year ten months, which is quite a long time. I wonder how he will be, for myself, I pray for discernment, compassion and love, he is a complex man, whenever I have seen him in the past, I have always been aware of pain, hopefully, after all, that has been written between us, we may arrive at a deeper level still.

3 October

Returned from London on 1 October to Holy Trinity, London SW7 to see M.I. I really did not know how he would be or what to expect. I was quite shocked when I first saw him, it is one year and ten months, so I would notice the change. He looked so frail physically and not well, his face was thinner and pale, he may well have been very tired, I kissed him and we sat down, side by side to talk, it was easy and words flowed between us. I learnt of the black depression that was upon him when he wrote the letter in question. I have never been aware of anybody, not only him, of the devastating effect this type of depression can have upon the whole person, one cannot possibly appreciate another's so deep pain unless it has been experienced oneself. This applies to everything, both physical, mental, emotionally and spiritually. He was very gentle in both speech and manner. Eucharist was at 11.45 am. I noticed how difficult it was for him to walk up the few steps to the altar. Afterwards, while I was waiting for him, I walked round the church…on the right-hand side about halfway down, there is a stone (I think) Pieta on the wall. The Pieta has always touched me at a deep level and this was no exception. He asked me if I would like to receive the blessing, I knelt at the altar rail, he placed his hands upon my head, the blessing was long, including many things, he then came round the altar rail and knelt beside me, we softly said the Lord's Prayer together, he ended with a final blessing. I was deeply moved, we talked a little longer, he walked with me to the church door, we stood briefly on the pavement, and the sun was shining brilliantly. I kissed him goodbye, he said, "May I kiss you?" I asked him if he was all right, he said he was, adding, "How do I look?"

"Tired," I answered. I left him with the sun shining on him…He is very concerned with death and firmly believes in hell, although not forever, but as a place of learning. I also believe this, but I think his views tend to be overshadowed by these times of deep depression. My belief is no less of a degree than his, but I am always conscious of subsequent light and the mercy and compassion of Our Lord and this overrides all else…I feel our friendship is at a deeper level still, within Christ, it has been severely tested – the test has been passed. Deo gratias.

26 November

I received a letter recently from M.I. He is still grieving for his friend. Later, my prayer reached new depths on his behalf and I was shown a great deal. In the early hours of the morning he phoned, I was extremely moved by his words and the obvious distress he was experiencing. This was to do with his deliverance work during which he is often attacked by evil forces. Later, during prayer for him, the words returned "Blessed is he who comes in the name of the Lord" for within this lies his freedom. The letter I had written to him, but hesitated to send, I now know would be right to send. His position, who he is, still on occasion gets in the way, but this has now all but disappeared. I recognise the need and must help if I am able to do so. He rang again at 12.40 pm!

1 December

Another letter from M.I. I am so glad I sent the letter, it was obviously the right thing to do. All is deepening.

4 December

Another letter from M.I. All is well, what I wrote apparently confirmed what he thought, there is a deep spiritual bond and now I have finally managed to get rid of the remaining bits of the 'dog collar', there will be no further uncertainties.

22 December

The words received on behalf of M.I. 'The Via Dolorosa' I decided to keep in the back of my mind and use on my next private retreat as the basis of meditation, but it was not to be. I no sooner received them, used them for the purpose they were given me, regarding M.I., than a meditation immediately began to form. It is now almost finished and I shall copy it in here. This has always happened to me ever since I began trying to put thoughts into words. I am unable to hold them back. The words come and I must write them down. Once this is done, they disappear from memory. I will phone M.I. before the 25th. Christmas is always a difficult and lonely time for him.

The Via Dolorosa

The road of pain and inner loneliness, at the core, lies faith that in God's time and when the earthly task is completed, faith will be justified and hope fulfilled in the love of Our Lord Jesus Christ. This is rather putting the end before the beginning, but the end must be visualised to enable us to walk that particular road at all. It is the road of pain as we seek to follow in the wake of Christ's pain as he trod it. There is a hymn "Oh Jesus! I have promised." etc. 'O let me see thy footmarks and in them plant mine own', these words should not be taken lightly. If we really intend to plant our own feet in them, then we must expect to be called upon to bear what we may see ourselves as incapable of bearing. Not all are called by God to tread this road, those who are so-called are usually those for whom God has a special mission, work to be done on his behalf and for which he has prepared us from the womb. We may be entirely unaware and are brought to it gradually over a long period of time until we are deemed strong enough to enter upon it, certainly never in our own strength, God is the source, and he alone bears us as we seek to fulfil his will. It may well be a considerable time before we realise we are called to tread so exactly in those sacred footprints. I believe at some point, as the road becomes progressively more difficult, it is fully realised. Christ's footprints were bloodied and those who tread in them will be bloodied too. Victory is preceded by suffering and fulfilment by traversing a hard road. In one sense, Christ's yoke is easy, one commits oneself and the journey begins. To commit oneself may be relatively easy, to walk in Our Lord's footsteps is not. As he trod the way of the Via Dolorosa, weakened as he was, a lonely and forsaken man, droplets of blood falling to the ground, leaving in their wake the outward signs of inner pain. Jesus did not ask Simon of Cyrene to carry his cross, he was ordered to do so by the soldiers. It does tic up with the fact that we are bidden to carry each other's burdens. Simon may well have resented being made to do this, yet he holds a place in history forever, an honour that went unrecognised. We do well to remember this when called upon to give help to someone we do not know but who is known to God as we are known to God. This is borne out by the legend of St Veronica, prompting us to show compassion to all in need. The imprint of Christ's face is upon all who are outcasts and rejected by mankind who does not see themselves as being the neediest of all. As Our Lord comes towards us, we are part of the crowd who watch his approach, he is bent with weariness and although he has relinquished the cross he walks as though he is still carrying it, its weight has moved from the physical to the inner man, he is bowed with grief and grief is heavy to bear. Inner tears fill the soul with such heaviness as to be almost unbearable, yet it was borne. His eyes are not on the ground but on the far horizon beyond which hope will be fulfilled. His eyes are of the utmost importance upon which to dwell. Eyes quite often speak when lips are silent, they are capable of reflecting the heart's desire and the soul's need without a word being spoken. The eyes of Christ were not upon the people lining the sides of the road but upon the known inner presence of his Father and towards the Holy Spirit who preceded him on his last earthly journey. Although suffering is clear to any who witness his obvious physical weakness and the mental and emotional strain so obvious on his face, yet as I face him as part of the crowd, I am aware of the clarity of his inner vision that overrides all else. His eyes reflect the purity of his soul, they reflect physical and mental pain too, for he is also a man and suffering in the same way as any man would suffer in the same circumstances. I believe this can be allied to his last agonising cry from the cross "My God, my God, why hast thou forsaken me?" Not the cry of God the Son, but the cry of a man to his Father. As he proceeds on his way, his whole being denotes failure, who among the crowd would look at him and see this as a prelude to victory? Although I have put myself in the position of being one of the crowd, I know the truth of the Resurrection. To those people, it would be an impossibility and laughable. The Son of God treads in the footsteps of man, the Son of Man lives in the truth that is God. Our Lord bearing his own cross (John 19, 17) symbolises the weight of man's sin, almost insupportable. I look again at the approaching figure nearing the end of the Via Dolorosa, am I the only one to 'see' that he does not travel alone? Myriads of the angelic host that accompany him on the way. He shows no awareness, can he be unaware? In one's own most dire need, are we always aware of support? Afterwards, the realisation may come but at the time, we may feel utterly alone and forsaken, pain can be so deep as to blot out any knowledge of those who uphold us. We are all in varying stages of learning the true meaning of faith, hope, and love. Those who have completed their own Via Dolorosa to its final conclusion recognise that it has not been in their own strength; with God, we can accomplish all that is good, without God, we are nothing. Again, I write that this probably sounds too simplistic, there are realms in which we can know nothing until we are within them, no matter how great our intellectual abilities, our theological learning, etc. No person on earth is privy to knowledge of God's eternal kingdom, one can only write/speak what is given within oneself. I have never been shown or understood that God the Father, Jesus the Son or the Holy Spirit is bound up with using complicated terminology to explain, unravel the mystery' of the Creator. It is a mystery and earth is not the place where it will be revealed. Perhaps I have accepted too easily, too readily, if I have, then it has never been at face value, only in the certain knowledge of God's indwelling. I have trodden my own Via Dolorosa, the end has not yet been reached. For those who have taken their own life I am sure of a special place within the love and mercy of God, for the mentally ill and mentally disabled too, they cannot be held responsible as those of sound mind are held responsible, all have been of value in the world and value cannot be judged on what the outer presence conveys, rather what has been taught to others through their contact with them, what has been learnt. All of us is for a purpose, nothing is discarded. The inner eye is returned to Our Lord, aware of his broken body, physical pain, his isolation amongst the throng. It is also aware of his far-seeing eye clouded as it is by inner loneliness that is often the deepest pain of all, yet, for all things that assailed him, his far-seeing eye beholds the horizon and beyond this, the fast-approaching hosts of heaven winging in as they await his imminent return.

24 December

Christmas Eve. I telephoned M.I. this morning and I am concerned, he spoke little and sounded so distressed, his voice was full of pain. I can do nothing but pray.

26 December

During this evening M.I. phoned, apparently he phoned yesterday too on Christmas Day, he spoke very freely and I knew by what he said and the sound of his voice that he was much better, fortunately; I phoned him when I did on Christmas Eve, although he said he felt a little better then, he knew he was being supported by prayer and it lifted him up. There is a great deal I could write here but it would not be wise to do so. I see him now clearly and I see my role clearly too. God certainly does use the most unexpected people.

1994

1 February

I had such a clear dream in the early hours of this morning concerning M.I. I am going to write anyway to see if we can meet in early July, so I will probably tell him of the dream. This is now late afternoon and I have written to M.I. I have told him the dream, he may be able to clarify it. I am copying here what I wrote.

"In the early hours of this morning, I had a dream concerning you and this is partly why I am writing to you today. It was as follows. I had an appointment to see you in London. I arrived early, you answered the bell and I came upstairs, the door was open, also the door of the room where you see people was open, I walked in, you were in your dressing gown, you looked quite well and was smiling. You said, 'I hoped you would not have been early, I didn't want you to know.' There were three men in the room who I assumed were doctors, I remember one very clearly he was about your height with dark hair and a moustache, he too was smiling, he said, "Dr Israel is ill and must go to the hospital, we are just making arrangements, I have told him he must not go out, but he insists that he must on, I looked at yon and said, 'You must not go out.' That was the end. It was a physical illness and what seems strange to me is that you were apparently so happy and not at all disturbed by it, it remains so clear." etc. I was shown what the illness was, but I did not tell him. If he asks, I suppose that I shall have to, I hope he does not! I have no doubt he will clarify it…I have been very undecided whether to travel to London again at all. I did tell myself that last year was the final year, yet the fact that I should go did not leave me. I prayed about this, especially to do with M.I. and knew that the effort must be made and I must go.

25 February

Received a phone call from M.I. He was attacked by Peruvian witch doctors. I was grateful it was 5.30 pm and not the middle of the night. We talked at length, constant reassurance that 'all will be well'. I cannot possibly know the effect these attacks have on him, I have never experienced this, but I am equally sure that to him it is reality. "I want you to tell me if you think I am wrong on any issue." The more I am involved with people, whoever they are, the more I am aware of 'certainly not me' – God.

5 March

Received a letter from M.I., much improved after his phone call, this friendship has developed in a way I would not have thought possible, a deeply spiritual bond.

1 March

I was sitting quietly with my eyes closed, M.I. conducts a Eucharist each Thursday morning at 11.45am. This fact entered my thoughts. I looked at the clock, it was 11.40am. I 'saw' him inwardly before the altar in the Lady Chapel at Holy Trinity, London, and held him in prayer.

1 July

A friend phoned and it was good to talk to him, especially regarding M.I. I have heard nothing, but D. is able to see him far more deeply than I do. About the 'inner man', I do see quite clearly, but whereas I want explanations regarding discourtesy, D accepts this as part of what he is. But shouldn't such people be called to book? Can they be unaware of how their behaviour affects others? We spoke of his 'deliverance work' and at what a cost this is to him. It did me much good to talk it all through.

12 July

M.I. rang tonight. I have come to the conclusion – perhaps a little late – that I am dealing with a very unstable man, very gifted, doing marvellous work regarding his deliverance work, another book that will come out early next year and which he says I shall be surprised to read, an auto-biographical one based on his own depression. We spoke at great length, but he sounded as though he was on a 'high', manic. I must remain stable to be able to cope. I had a bad night but all is well now (the following day, 13th) and I do not doubt that I shall sleep well tonight (14th). He asked me if I realised that many suffering from these depressions commit suicide. I said, "Yes, I did realise it."

He said, "I shall never do that."

I replied, "No, you won't." When I said, "If you feel our relationship has run its course, then tell me."

He answered, "Our relationship will never run its course, it will continue into eternity." What a strange and complex man he is, what I have to do is to keep him on course as it were, keep his head above water. He is doing what I had written to him, some time ago regarding the death of his friend, that perhaps no one else would be given to him to take over her role and it would now be between himself and God, apparently since doing this 'all is well', but all sounded very far from well as I listened to him. He went back to the time when I left London in January 1991, that he had been on the edge of darkness and I had deserted him, but I was very firm on this, the decision to move here had proved to be the right one, that there were people here that I felt I was predestined to meet and this would not have happened if I had remained in E17. In any case, the time would have come there that I would not have been able to travel to SW10 alone, much less for any other reason as I grew older. It actually does become easier for me as we go on because I am learning all the time and the 'dog collar' does not hold me back as it has done earlier, neither does his position. I do, however, respect who he is. He wanted reassurance that I still prayed for him daily, he emphasised that everyone told him how well he looked, his prayer life was wonderful, his church flourished, everyone there loved him, his conducting of retreats went from strength to strength, his voice, as he spoke, was higher than usual with many little attacks of what I can only describe as 'giggling'. His remarks regarding 'friend' caused me to smile inwardly! Since speaking to 'friend' last week I have been able to remove any 'self' from my prayer for him, 'self must be removed if prayer is to be effective and this is not easy when one is involved on a personal level.' So, at this point, I am, refreshed and go on.

17 July

My thoughts returned to M.I. again and I remembered something very important, towards the end of his phone call I said to him, "Whatever darkness you feel is overtaking you, you must remember that God is within you."

He replied in his normal voice and without hesitation, "and I am within God." This is something we should all remember, whatever circumstances we are in. I feel that this was a fitting end to the conversation between us, it brought me to the realisation of the truth and brought him back from the edge of darkness to the ever-abiding knowledge of 'Christ within'. How true it is that we should not worry about what we should say, when the time comes we shall be given it.

19 August

Received an answer (from M.I.) this morning regarding a certain priest X, it was exactly as I expected it to be, a very definite "No." In one sense, I absolutely agree with him, although his words "I hope this subject does not arise again," tend to send me in the opposite direction, but I do know that is my temperament. Fortunately, D.B.T. will be here next Monday and before I show him M.I.'s letter, I shall ask his opinion too. One asks, but it does not mean that one will follow it, whoever they are. Whatever decision I make, it will involve a long talk with X if I decide to do it, anyway. Our Lord will give or withhold, I cannot see why he should not be asked, it is not something one asks for lightly and one must examine the motive. I will give it further thought, holding it before Our Lord and see what transpires on Monday.

(The issue here is a request from X for the laying on of hands by Ivy for the possible transference of spiritual gifts)

22 August

D was so helpful regarding X and all it entailed, he does agree that if I do what has been proposed above, bearing in mind (to be effective) it must be the will of God and, as I have written, "Our Lord will either give or withhold," I shall say nothing to M.I. unless he asks. His answer came so quickly, he must have read my letter and answered it immediately! Considering that he had returned from holiday only that morning and the postmark was 11am.

(There is no evidence whether Ivy in the end did what was asked for.)

4 December

Returned last night from London, The time with M.I. was good, much was talked about and all is well.

6 December

I had been puzzled as to the reason M.I. showed me his bedroom. Very few people have been allowed to see it. That I should have seen the room and perhaps be given something on a spiritual level concerning it that would hold some meaning. Later this morning, however, another thought was given. It is always in the early hours of the morning that he is attacked by evil, darkness, witch-doctors etc, so knowing this, I can use my prayer for him in a more constructive manner regarding the fact that he is always in that bed and in that room when he is thus invaded. I am very glad to have been shown this. Also, on the wall by the bedhead, not above it but by the side of it, is the most beautiful crucifix. This too is so relevant to him calling for God to relieve him and which I believe is happening.

1995

18 May

I have finished M.I.'s book 'Dark Victory'. I do wonder what many people will make of it that do not know him on a personal level. He has been very open regarding himself and depression, most of what he has written is already known to me, and also I have been able to tie updates when his depressions have made him seem unreasonable. I have found a reference to myself on p. 150, the chapter on 'The confluence of darkness and light', the death of his aged friend who was on a psychic level with him, he writes, "She was 93 years old and was active until the time that a massive heart attack killed her after 10 days gallant fight." So far, I have found no replacement, and a very wise friend has told me that I never shall; "God alone will be my partner now," etc., he depended on her and I do believe that this dependence should end with her death, although he does believe that she is still helping him from 'the other side.' Towards the end of this book a thought entered my head, I remembered Julian of Norwich and the vision she had of Our Lord showing her a small round object resembling a hazelnut, in this she saw three truths, "he made it, he loves it, he sustains it" and this is certainly what has happened in M.I.'s life, in many other lives, of course, it really is food for thought when we take time to consider how God does work in one's life. There are things he has written that I do not believe in and some that leave a doubt. But there is no way he could possibly have done this work unless God had loved him and sustained him throughout his painful life.

24 November

M.I. is seriously ill in hospital with pneumonia, there is a person on the answerphone in his flat "No message, no cards, no gifts, no visits." Well, that is typical of him, I have been in touch with D.B.T. who knew nothing about it, will phone the flat tomorrow to see if there is any further news. The voice said there would be a bulletin between 24–26 November. My prayers are for him, he has told me more than once that he wishes to die. I know that he really meant that, they were not just passing words because he was depressed, also that he would die before me and would be waiting to greet me. For all his work in many areas, he is a tormented soul that nothing in this world can heal.

25 November

Phoned M.I.'s flat, he is much improved, "Please, no cards, messages, etc. It is hoped he is well enough to convalesce next week, next bulletin 2–3 December. I do wonder how emotional he is.

21 December

The shortest day, bitterly cold. I have received a Christmas card from M.I. but he has forgotten to sign it.

1996

1 February

I have finished M.I.'s book on Angels. I should say it is like the curate's egg, good in parts. I am glad not to have spent £9.99 on it myself. Nevertheless, some of it was good, some repetition too, from his previous book 'Dark Victory'. I wonder if some authors realise they do this or if it is deliberate. One thing I found irritating was his reference to his redundancy from medical work, he writes he was "prompted by an angel to become a full-time priest" and not to stay as an NSM, this is against the better judgment of his friends. I distinctly remember seeing him at this time and saying to him that the call to full-time priesthood was what he should do, also writing to him along those lines. He was, at this time, in an extremely low and depressed state. I don't suppose that this is deliberate on his part, but using the 'angel' as his prod was to be far more effective to his readers than the suggestion of an ordinary human being. He has done this at least once before, to my knowledge regarding infant souls after death. Perhaps I should give him the benefit of the doubt?

30 September

Received a letter from Martin Israel, which momentarily threw me, I did not recognise the writing until I looked at it through a magnifying glass and knew it was his. It sounds as though he is suffering from Parkinson's disease or motor neurone. He has been dismissed from his church because of his infirmities. D.B.T. knew nothing of this and was going to check. He thinks it would be good and bring him comfort if I could see him. This could be arranged in mid-November, I hesitate to phone him, he is so unpredictable in his reactions. Must wait and see what D.B.T. can discover. Martin has suffered so much literally throughout his life.

1 October

D.B.T. phoned last evening regarding Martin Israel, he was made to resign a month ago and cannot now leave home unaided. He has a full-time carer, he suggests that I write to him and ask whether he would like to see me if I can manage to get to London, so I must do this. It is not going to be an easy letter to put together, but the words I know will be given to me.

19 November

Here I am back at home after my stay in London, a very eventful three days. On Saturday afternoon, I went to see M.I. I expected for some reason to find him even thinner, but he has put on so much weight and his face is red and quite bloated, probably due to the medication. I am so grateful, I prayed for him at 3.30 pm on Saturday. I was really uplifted and supported by this, words were given to me to say to him, tears ran down his face when I arrived. "I never thought I would see you again." His hands tremble all the time, he forgets words, etc, but we communicated with each other without difficulty, much was said between us that stays between us. He has a wheelchair now and hobbles is the word, rather than walks. He insisted on getting on his feet when I was leaving because he wanted me to kiss him! The arrangement is that I call him at 9.45 am on any morning, and he will do the same. It remains to be seen if I am able to see him again, he wants to but I told him that I cannot promise, much depends on my own health and getting a lift down. He does not seem to understand this. I am glad to have had the opportunity to see him and also D.B.T. with whom I stayed. D, A and I had much to catch up on, it is so easy to just continue as though we had met yesterday…many, many thanks to God.

29 November

I telephoned M.I. as arranged at 9.45 am every morning. I think he is probably in a state of depression again, his answers were monosyllabic, to say the least, and the conversation between us was under one minute. I do find it difficult to deal with, one can never foresee how he will be. I think there is a certain amount of anger in me that should not be there at all. I will phone again on 20 December…unless he keeps his word and phones me as he also arranged when we met. I must remember at all times how ill he is. It isn't as though I don't realise his difficult temperament. I've known him long enough to accept this and must take it in my stride and get on with it.

1997

28 January

M.I. rang this morning, we had a long talk, I do find it difficult to believe that the doctors' specialists do not know what is wrong, bearing in mind that he too is a doctor and pathologist. I rather think he must know but does not want to say. If this is true, then I do understand his reasons. It is possible he has not accepted it. Once it has been put into words, it becomes a reality, the truth is the one we are not always ready to face. Although Prinknash is associated with Burnham Abbey OSB, he has never been there. It is not too far from here and would be possible for me to go there if he was there, so it may happen. I was glad he phoned, he said, "We owe each other a great deal." That is true.

29 January

I received an insight regarding M.I. that I must pass on to Christopher and then leave it to him to make a decision. It has arisen from something I said to Martin and which I now understand as important.

3 February

I spoke to Christopher yesterday regarding M.I. and he is willing to do it, i.e. give M.I. the laying on of hands if he wants to receive this, we spoke at length. I have written to M.I. and must wait now to hear his reaction. I have kept a copy of the letter so there can be no misunderstanding.

5 February

M.I. contacted C, he had lost my phone number. Pauline called me and I contacted him. He sounded very unwell, had a very bad day yesterday because of a serious epileptic attack. This is another area where Christopher will be able to help him because he has travelled that road. M.I. wants him to minister to him and said he was given an insight concerning this a long time ago. This was almost what C. said to me about himself, he showed no surprise when I asked him. M.I. sees a specialist tomorrow and it depends on this when he and C can meet. We talked a great deal, but what it really amounts to, is his need and reassurance that I love him. I gave him this unreservedly, in Our Lord – I do. I cannot remember when it was that I was shown all that is happening now, and wrote to him to tell him that. It was nothing to do with his work, but a physical illness and this has proved to be true. God has given me so much.

2 March

M.I. rang, there is a great improvement in his health, he has dismissed his doctors (Harley Street) saying they were only after his money and for me to be wary of the medical profession (what does he expect me to do if I am ill?) He is not now having his knee operated on. He is getting about much better, although it is still painful. He asked why I thought he had to suffer so much. I suspected that he may have had to learn a lesson, he agreed, saying, "Humility, I have always lacked humility." Did his voice sound stronger? I said it did, and, he added "Full of joy." He is conducting a retreat in Glastonbury and will be able to preside at the Eucharist. He must, however, keep his carer as this is necessary. He said his improvement is a miracle! Prayer is of the essence and must continue.

6 March

M.I. said he was conducting a retreat at Glastonbury this week. I am very interested in knowing how he coped, but probably never shall. He only seems to contact me when in distress, not when all is going well.

30 April

M.I. is 70 years old today. He wrote to me not too long ago that he doubted he would live to see his 70th birthday!

28 May

I rang M.I. as I had heard nothing from him since late March. The carer answered, a young Australian man who I saw when I last visited Martin in November 1996. Not good news, he finally had the operation on his knee, but the anaesthetic had a very bad effect on him. He is totally confused and now incontinent. I asked if he knew what was wrong, as M had told me the doctors could not agree. The carer laughed and said, "It is senile dementia." These were his words, not Alzheimer's disease, but it is one and the same. I was shocked, this had not entered me along the lines of Parkinson's or motor neurone disease. I left my name and telephone number. He promised to phone and let me know how he is or if anything untoward happens. At present, he is unable to see or speak to anyone. My prayer now is for his release from suffering. Such a brilliant mind. It is not death, is it, but the process of dying, Martin spoke of this last November. He said he couldn't wait to go. This was not in any morbid sense at all, it is in a sense how I feel myself. However, unless we take our own life, there is no option but to wait and use our remaining time here for good purposes. I would like to see him, but there is no point, he would not know me.

He said to me a long time ago regarding my death, "How the trumpets will sound?" which made me laugh whenever I remembered, but now? I hope the trumpets will sound for him and that it will be soon…He told me before I left London in January 1991, he would die first.

I remember saying, "I am nine years older than you."

"Yes," he said, "nevertheless I shall die before you and shall be waiting to greet you." Many things he said to me privately bring comfort now, Song of Songs Ch. 8 "Place me like a seal over your heart, for love is as strong as death."

1 June

Whilst holding Martin in prayer, I saw that his physical body is withdrawing from this world. While this is taking place, and who but God can know how long this will be, may his soul be nourished, be taught and prepared for his entering into eternal life. I could almost 'hear' his voice agreeing. I pray that he will not be held too long here. I have begun writing 'Martin, the inner man.'

3 June

Martin

The inner man is in many ways a tormented man, completely faithful to Our Lord and his teaching and yet running parallel to this knew himself surrounded by an evil that constantly probed him, tormented him, seeking to overcome him and grind him down, a brilliant mind, insight into other people's minds that was disconcerting. Quietly spoken, penetrating eyes that literally stripped one bare. A lonely man, the first time I had an appointment with him, August 1974, he said after a long silence, "What do you see?"

"Loneliness," I answered without hesitation.

"Yes," he said. I had reached him immediately and there was no turning back. I had three appointments in quick succession, i.e. August, September, December 1976, then at three-monthly intervals. Quite early on he said, "I am not able to direct you, you are to be directed by the Holy Spirit." And so the way was opened for friendship. Looking back, I realise that I had accepted what he had said, but at the same time, I was detached. This is difficult to explain, it was as though it was someone else in this position, not me, and it was a very slow process of unfolding. Each time I saw him, I was acutely aware of his penetrating eyes, however, I did not turn away. These moments of unspoken thoughts, of silence, spoke of a 'sharing' that needed no words. In friendships of depth, silences are often more eloquent than the spoken word. Each time before I left, we shared 10–15 minutes of silent prayer. He never omitted to say "Thank you." Neither of us spoke of what we had received or prayed for, but for me, they almost always bore fruit. I finally came to the conclusion that I was drawing away from him. He suffered periodically from what I believe was clinical depression. One of the most serious was when he was made redundant from the Royal College of Surgeons, he was in a suicidal frame of mind. Although he reassured me afterwards that he would not have taken his own life, who can say? He was at this time an NSM at Holy Trinity Church, Prince Consort Road SW7.

I can understand the feeling of rejection, but as I pointed out, he could now give all his time to a full-time ministry. He became priest-in-charge and his work on retreats, counselling, exorcism and writing escalated. He became much sought after. It was a very long time before he spoke to me regarding certain aspects of his work. Much of what he said I did not understand. He assumed that I did, but I did not. Nothing that he said in this respect affected me at all, I remembered them but did not dwell on them or on any implication of evil they might hold. Looking back again, I see this as a grace bestowed, for much damage could otherwise have been done. This work drained him utterly, combined with everything else he was involved in. He never ceased to pray, whatever the circumstances. Prayer to him is lifeblood; he never relinquished it. He was never able to see himself as a formidable man and was always surprised when he learnt this from various sources. I don't believe he suffered fools gladly and had little or no appetite for social graces, much less for small talk. He spoke of marriage and the loss he experienced by making a decision early on to remain celibate. "It would have had to be a very understanding lady," he said, an understatement if ever there was one. I have no doubt whatsoever there were queries among clergy and lay people alike regarding his sexuality, I have no reason to doubt he was heterosexual. When I first met him he was anti-homosexual but he changed his views and about 1994 wrote an excellent article in their favour. He sent a copy to me, I passed it on to a priest in this area. I rather wish I had kept it. In the late '80s, signs of ill health began to appear, once or twice at intervals, suicide was mentioned. The last time, earlier this year, there again, he said he would not do it. As time went on, he opened up more and more. I was truly amazed when he spoke of his low self-esteem. I must have shown this, because he said, "That has surprised you." It had coupled with this, "I have always lacked humility." Many things he disclosed showed me he was aware of his failings. As far as I am aware, he did not have a confessor and after various let downs early in his ministry said, he would never trust a man again. He came late to the priesthood, ordained in 1975, one year before I met him. In the whole of his life, there have been dark shadows hovering in the background and many times, they have overwhelmed him. There has always been gentleness in his manner towards me, he said I understood him. I don't know that is the correct word, but I did see it clearly below the surface. It is a two-way friendship, which is how it should be, what I found difficult earlier was to accept our very different backgrounds, or to understand how two such different people could be brought together. This was probably because of my own history and a very real fear of rejection, I came slowly to realise we each supplied a need for the other. He was born in South Africa on 30 April 1927, an only child brought up in his early life by Ayahs. He did not know the meaning of parental love any more than I have done. He regarded his mother as a butterfly

In December, the meeting of 1976, he told me of his father, then around 89–90 years old and still living in South Africa. He thought he should make the journey to see him, at the same time he hesitated, he did not want to go. Bearing in mind this was only the third time I had seen him, I said, "I think you should go, he may die at any time and you could regret not seeing him."

He did go and said when I next saw him that much had been achieved. His father died sometime later. Quite a long time after that, he told me, "All is well." He believed in the 'bridge' between this world and the next and that reconciliation was a reality between those here and those there, something I have never forgotten. Very early he said, I must always speak the truth to him about himself. This can be a difficult issue because when people ask for truth, it is not always what they want to hear, as I have written before, truth and love go together. Truth without love can be very harsh indeed, love without truth is really a mask of the meaning of the word 'love', an often-misunderstood word. During these past months of deteriorating health, he needed reassurance that he was loved, to respect someone is not necessarily to love them. For all he gave as a priest, counsellor, within the work of exorcism, not forgetting his many books, his own need never abated. I doubt he ever asked for help, when at one point I suggested he receive the laying on of hands, he said, "There is nobody I would ask, but you are here, you do it," and without further ado put a chair in the centre of the room and sat on it. In many respects, he was not approachable on a personal level, any who attempted to 'get to know him' got short shrift. This is understandable and often a necessity for those in the public eye. His closest friend died some years ago on 30 April, Martin's confident, a good and holy man, a man of integrity. Another friend, a very elderly lady who lived in the West Country and was obviously on his wavelength regarding exorcism and the forces of evil died about 2–3 years ago. This was not a personal friendship as such but concerned only with his work in that field. He depended on her being available at any hour he phoned, often in the early hours of the morning, he spoke to me about her after her death and said, "Would there be a replacement?"

I answered, "Probably not, it was now between him and God alone and on God, he should depend." He replied that these were his own thoughts, he had needed them to be confirmed. She was not replaced. Memories crowd in now of things he has said to me over the years. I have recently learnt that he has Senile Dementia, Alzheimer's disease. I feel bereaved and pray for his release from such suffering. At first, I could only think of the cruelty of such an illness, but last Thursday, 31 May, was the feast of Corpus Christi, during the Eucharist, as I held him before God, words filtered through that were said to me many years ago by Fr Reginald Smith CR concerning someone in a similar mental state. She collapsed suddenly and there followed a four-month period of deterioration until finally, she was 'like a cabbage'.

This worried me, I talked to Fr Smith who simply said, "In the end, she had to learn." And this is how I have been able to come to terms with Martin's situation. In the end, we all have to learn. I understand it as a final stripping away, peeling off the layers as his soul, irrespective of his physical body, is nourished and prepared before leaving the world for the life to come.

Before I left London, early 91, he said, "I shall die before you." I queried this as I am 9 years older than he is. He smiled, "I shall die before you and will be waiting to greet you." It is still possible for it to happen the other way round, but only God knows. We shall see. I think there was a need for me to write this – my need perhaps a therapy?

Regarding what I wrote above about Alzheimer's, I learnt later that it was Parkinson's disease.

18 July

I rang London this morning to ask after M.I. He is in hospital but the drugs are working and it looks more hopeful. When I said, "Is there a possibility he may come out of this?" The carer asked what I meant. "He has senile dementia," I said, "You told me when I last rang."

"I never told you that." The long and the short of it is that this carer is not the same as the one I spoke to before. They are both New Zealanders, not Australian, I was not able to tell the difference on the phone. This one, Cliff, said that the other, Mike, had drawn his own conclusions, but they were wrong, it is Parkinson's disease.

I suppose that Parkinson's Disease is the lesser of two evils. It is not satisfactory to be told two different diagnoses, but there is no way of checking, prayer continues.

29 August

Wonderful news this morning, I phoned M.I. and was given a different number. I phoned this number and was amazed when Martin answered it, clearly and his old self. He has moved, there were very difficult stairs at Tregunter Road which made it impossible for him. We had a long talk, it is Parkinson's disease, coupled with epilepsy and a condition where no apparent cause can be found. At any time he loses consciousness, it is not to do with epilepsy, he is bodily crippled but mentally has fully recovered. He said, "I have been to hell and am now a Christian, I am a changed person, I no longer judge, my disposition has gentled." I have his new address, so I can write and phone him. He said how dependent he had been and still was, on prayer. The most important person in his life at the moment is his N.Z. carer, Cliff. He said, "He is wonderful." I have spoken to him on the phone and it was he who gave me the correct diagnosis as opposed to Malcolm's Alzheimer's. I really do mean it when I say, "Thanks be to God." One other remark, "I am no longer ashamed of my past." I am not sure in what context he meant that?

17 September

I was pleased and surprised, this morning to receive M.I.'s latest book by the courtesy of the publishers, "Doubt, the way of growth." I knew there were two further books in the pipeline some months ago but had not realised M. had got this far. On the front cover is a painting by William Blake, Satan smiting Job with boils. I know that Job is Martin's favourite book in the Old Testament, considering all things, how applicable this is. I phoned to thank him, he said he was a little better, he did sound very tired, his voice was weak.

28 September

I (have) read M.I.'s book, I think the last two chapters were the best, these did 'speak to me'. Much of it was repetition – he did say some time that "You only write one book." In chapter 6, he refers to himself as a cripple, I do not like the term! "What does it matter if I can't walk so long as I can help people!"

referring I am sure to himself. In a different walk of life, he would feel quite differently regarding not being able to walk. I do 'see through' some of what he writes. Simply because I know him, I can 'see' him, sitting in his chair and 'hear' him speaking. Time and again, he advocates, "Be still, quiet, dismiss everything from your mind and you will become aware of the presence of God within, listen to him." etc. Absolutely true, but not easy to achieve, it is at the very point of being still, inactive, when those with varying problems, who deliberately lead over-busy lives to blot them out, find that when they are still, all rush back in with a vengeance. It takes a very long time to learn to be still, to empty oneself that we may be filled. Some of what he writes comes over to me as arrogant, although I am sure he would not recognise it as being so. Nevertheless, I have enjoyed reading it and it makes no difference to my affection for him.

25 October

Returning a book to the bookcase, I found a memoir by Fr. Geoffrey Curtis CR, who was M.I.'s closest friend before he died (*He*) has quoted some lines by T.S.Eliot which are very meaningful to me and I know will also be to M.I. "That the dead had no speech, for when living they can tell you being dead; the communication of the dead is tongued with fire beyond the language of the living."

1998

17 February

I rang to M.I. this morning and spoke to the carer. He is so much improved, walking well and taking up his work again, improved in all areas of his life. Tomorrow, he is off to Barbados, incredible, I think now he can be removed from the prayer lists he is on. As far as I am concerned, I shall remember him myself. He may telephone me this afternoon. If he does, 'all is well' if he does not, 'all is well'.

It is now late afternoon and M.I. has telephoned. He said how moved he was to hear me! He will be away for 18 days and will let me know after his return if he feels well enough to be taken off the prayer lists, so I was wrong in thinking otherwise. It was good to hear from him again.

26 April

Martin telephoned today after quite a lapse, he is very well and now out of the wheelchair, something he said he never thought would happen, he is also in the process of writing another book, "Happiness and something about evil." I cannot remember his exact words but it is based on what he called 'my year in hell'. He would like to see me, but there is no way I can get there under my own steam, especially as the new address is 'London SW11', but as he said, "If it is meant to be, then it will be." I promised I would not lose touch and assured him, as he asked, I would remember him on his birthday on 30 April, and he will be 71 years old. One typical 'Martin' remark, he said, "You are nine years older than me."

"Yes," I answered, "but not so wise."

"Oh you will be," he said! With that thought, what else can I say? I have to write to him on time for his birthday.

2 May

A short letter from M.I. in response to the card and enclosed poem for him on his birthday. I write this because I must record the clarity of his writing, showing the tremendous improvement in his health. He writes, "It is a pity that a collection of your poems cannot be printed." Hopefully one day, it will.

30 May

I was amazed to receive an answer from M.I. today. He could only have received my letter yesterday. He writes that his own improvement in health continues apace, he has been for a walk in Battersea Park, just under a mile from his home, SW11...I think coincidence is not the right word, how wonderfully does the Holy Spirit work...

12 August

Received a wonderful letter from M.I. in answer to another I wrote to him last week. At the risk of repeating myself, "I never cease to be amazed at the people God brings together." His comments regarding my vicar (After reading his letter in the church magazine) had me in fits of laughter. I never at any time ever saw him as a 'delightful man', I shall 'see' him with a new vision next Sunday.

20 August

Received a further letter from M.I. clarifying the meaning of the meditation I sent him. Very good for me to read, mark, learn and inwardly digest.

9 September

Received a letter from M.I. regarding the dream concerning him last January. It is interesting to read his interpretation of it, some words about himself and me that I do not go along with, but I have to remember his lack of self-esteem, which he has talked to me about in the past.

1999

17 April

Received directly from publishers of M.I.'s book 'Happiness that lasts'.

26 April

Have finished reading M.I.'s book, very interesting, especially the autobiographical description of his illness, he is much more forthcoming on a personal level than he has been before in print. A few things are different to those he has told me and written to me, but bearing in mind the type of illness he has been through, this is not to be wondered that M.I. will be 72 years this coming Friday, I have enclosed with his card a short note regarding chapter one of his book because much of what he has written after he emerged from his illness regarding 'letting go', 'what will be, will be', 'unconcern for the future', I have written in this book in January-February when I was bidden just 'To Be'!

1 July

Today, the funeral of Ann Harrison (mother of a former vicar 'of St Michael's, Walthamstow) remembered her in prayer as I had promised Ian I would do. (*See the opening experience of water in a chapter of this book.*) At midday, received the phone call from M.I., he sounded so weary and exhausted, he so wanted, he said, "To go over to the other side where I shall find happiness." Apparently, while in Barbados, he had a stomach haemorrhage that he said was because of the drugs he had been put on. He has one of them now. I just got the feeling from what he said and the way he spoke that he had had literally enough. We spoke of a further book (the Spirit leads me to this!) but I shall be surprised if it materialises, although I did say that I would pray to this end, but it will very much be 'if it is thy will, O Lord'. He rang off quite suddenly, almost mid-sentence. He said he remembered Ann Harrison, but I doubt this. One very positive thing Martin said was, "My prayer life has not deteriorated in any way and that is the most important thing I can do."

20 November

Received a letter from M.I. regarding the poem I sent him that I wrote at Hemingford Grey. I am flattered by his words but am well aware that whatever I write is 'given' to me. He is going to New Zealand in November for a month to try to escape some of the winter. His walking is improving and his writing (i.e. his letter writing) is back to normal.

2000

18 February

I decided to phone M.I. as I expected a letter from him which did not arrive. He sounded so frail, he said how wonderful New Zealand had been, but when he returned mid-January, he had pneumonia and was in the hospital for two weeks, also an operation for piles, 'very uncomfortable'. He has had many fits which he said are always triggered off by an infection of any kind. The type of epilepsy he has is the 'temporal lobe'. Apparently, afterwards, he unintentionally upsets people, but he cannot ever remember doing this. He is having to put people in the picture more so they will understand. In two days, he is going to Barbados again for two weeks, so hopefully, this will do him some good. He has just finished writing another book, 'Learning to love'. It is written in conjunction with somebody else, he told me the name but I have forgotten it. I told him of the incident in the chapel (Christopher) on Christmas Day, regarding Susan and her epileptic seizure and how this remained within me and the words given to me were as followed, "In the midst of human frailty – I am." This touched him deeply as I knew it would. I suggested he remember them. His final words were, "We are never far apart."

6 March

M.I. phoned, he has returned from Barbados and obviously wanted to talk about himself. His voice was much stronger than two weeks ago. The Parkinson's is under control at the moment and the epileptic seizures have abated a little. Much of what he said regarding himself I cannot disclose, but it is really amazing what he is prepared to disclose and how he 'sees' himself.

4 May

M.I. phoned, he is much stronger and sounded much improved. His book 'Learning to love', comes out in December, so a little while to go yet. It is based on those who do not have faith, who are not Christians. His two carers, both young New Zealand men, have "nothing to do with Christianity." I suggested that perhaps they should read it! He spoke again regarding 'his longing to go' and at the same time reminded me of what I had said some time ago, "Your work is not finished." He spoke on many other things which are not for recording here, a long phone call but good to know that he is much improved, people are coming to see him again and for exorcism too. I really do appreciate his friendship and yet I feel completely detached from it…

23 September

M.I. telephoned, we had a long conversation, it was the anniversary of his Ordination on 21 September, St Matthew's Day. He is holding his own regarding Parkinson's, although as he said, "It is taking its toll," but his speech is clear and he can still work a little with help. His life now he says, "is prayer." I would very much like to see him, but it is not possible, I do know my limitations and memories are clear…

2001

6 March

Received Martin Israel's latest book from the publisher this morning. I thought it came out last December, but it is 2001. It is called 'Learning to love'. I look forward to reading it and must write to thank him. I thought he had forgotten. Obviously not. The cover strikes a note immediately within me, mostly blue with a white dove in flight in the centre.

9 March

The chapters of M.I.'s book 'Learning to love' are relatively short. I have read two so far and I realise I shall have to re-read the whole book once I have finished it. Already there are two things he has written that I am at odds with. This book is written in conjunction with 'Neil Broadbent'. Why this is I don't know but I am wondering about influence, we shall see.

20 September

Martin Israel rang. It is the anniversary of his Ordination tomorrow (St Matthew). He sounded so much better, he had been for a long walk this morning and there was so much improvement. He is now writing poetry and hopes to get it published. He will send me some, so that will prove interesting, his poetry rhymes – it is not blank verse! It was good to hear from him. He said he would like to live to be my age – 83 years – I said, "If you do, I shall be 92 years, if this happens then we must meet." This caused laughter and he is not usually given to laughter!

4 October

Received a letter/card from M.I. in reference to what I had sent him, regarding the terrorist attack in America on 11 September. He thanked me for my poem 'The wounded world' and says he has written a poem too and has called it 'An act of barbarity 11 September'. It consists of seven flowing sonnets! What can one say to that? (I note that he has not sent me a copy) Seriously, I would like to have read it.

2002

16 February

Received most unexpectedly this morning Martin Israel's latest book, 'The devout life', based on selected extracts from William Law's writings and his psychology of mysticism…he told me some time ago that he had written a book of poetry, but this cannot be it!

12 June

Having not heard a word from M.I. for some little time, I telephoned him yesterday. I wanted to know how he was because of intercessory prayer. His voice was so weak I could barely hear him at all. I did not stay on the phone for long, I did not wish to tire him. Parkinson's disease, MS and motor neurone seem such cruel illnesses to suffer from. It is such a long time before it runs its course and they are freed at last.

11 July

The word 'equanimity' has been in and out of my mind for several days. Many years ago when visiting M.I. he used the expression to whatever it was I had asked him, "Equanimity in all things." It was a new thought to me at that time, it is also something I have never forgotten.

23 December

For some time on and off, there have been times of what M.I. used to call 'malaise'. This was coupled with an inner feeling of an almost 'not caring' that seemed to overwhelm me, a 'what does it matter?' etc, relieved from time to time by the return of 'Light'. Such a period overwhelmed me recently, an almost depressed feeling, and I am not given to depression! This has not prevented me from praying but prayer was almost automatic.

2004

8 September

I shall send him an anniversary ordination card and a short letter. If there is no response, then I can only conclude he is not capable now of communicating, I see no other explanation!

24 September

I received an answer from M.I. today. I am so glad to have heard from him. He says he is now severely incapacitated and in a wheelchair but his spirit is joyful.

1 November

I am re-reading one of M.I.'s books 'Healing as Sacrament' today. On finishing chapter 9 called 'The gift of healing', my thoughts turned to Martin, his work, his present physical health for which there is no known cure. Our friendship over so many years and the living Spirit within him throughout this. I asked God for words to send to him. I had no doubts whatsoever they would be given, they were. I copy them here and will send them to him.

Within the deepest recesses of my soul,
Thy Spirit lives.
Bodily ills may affect me,
Pain, an integral part of my life,
But within the deepest recesses of my soul,
Thy Spirit lies.
I ask not why such physical ills afflict me,
I ask not for a miracle of healing,
I ask not, because within the deepest recesses of my soul,
Thy Spirit lives.
Thou art there that I may draw sustenance,
Spiritual food sustains my need.
Thy Body and Blood my daily Bread.
Thanks be to thee, my Lord Jesus Christ,
Within the deepest recesses of my soul,
Thy Spirit lives.

2005

30 April

Today is M.I.'s 79th birthday. Prayer continues, it is such a long drawn out illness. I have no way of knowing how he is. If I do phone him the carer just says "I will pass on the message." So many memories rise to the surface.

2007

27 October

Around 12.30, the vicar phoned and asked if I knew that Martin had died 2–3 days ago. I was amazed, I was not sad but joyful that at last his long road of pain had finally ended and he had left this life behind him. I remember a long time ago Martin said to me, "I shall die before you and when you come, I shall be waiting to greet you." I was born April 1918, he was born April 1927. He has been held my in prayers daily for a long time, but for a few days recently there has been not only a strong feeling but an almost certainty that his life in this world was drawing to a close. 'Thanks be to thee, O Lord.' All is indeed well with him now.

29 October

Today the following came very quickly, with no hesitation at all.
A close friend died recently,
Memories come flooding back,
One remains clear, I hear his voice.
"I shall die before you and when you come, I shall be
There to welcome you."
Does this beg the question regarding life after death?
The body dies – the soul – the essence of life lives on.
Our Lord rose from the dead – he lives.
We too shall live within the Eternal Light – the
Light of Christ.
We too shall welcome those we love,
Death is not something to be feared.
It is the door through which we pass into Eternal Life.
Martin died on 30 October.
(In fact, he died on 23 October. Ivy has written this on 27 October!)

Interestingly, Ivy never refers to Martin again in her writing, not even details of his funeral. In less than a year later, on 8 August 2008, she writes the last entry in her spiritual diary. Her health was failing but there is also a sense that with Martin's death, something has gone out of her life.

Sadly, Ivy destroyed many of Martin's letters because she felt that they contained things too personal for them to be seen by a wider readership. However, looking at the evidence in their remaining correspondence, we can discover how her diary notes above interrelate with his understanding of their friendship from his side. Here follows the 45 letters that survive.

6 December 1978

Dear Ivy,

Thank you for your letter. I think to myself that the correct interpretation of your vision was that Our Lord came down himself to bring his Mother back to his Father. The actual time is irrelevant – indeed, it is an eternal action, for Our Lady is not only Queen of Heaven but also our great intercessor. To intercede means to be able to identify yourself with the ones you are praying for. This is what I have learned in my daily intercessions for the Nazis. So Our Lady is also one of us.

I saw my father in July-August. God knows whether I shall see him again in the flesh. But I do not expect him to die yet. He is a very resilient old man with a great will to live. May he be granted some years of happy life yet in full command of his faculties.

I'm glad you will be coming to Pleshey, in July. Let us pray it is a good retreat. Thank you once more for the picture.

With love,

Martin.

2 January 1981

Dear Ivy,

Thank you for sharing the important message that came to you about those who have passed beyond this mortal life. I know it is true and your source is of divine origin. My father and I are at peace (Shalom – the peace of Christ). I wish you all blessings for this year. I am glad you will be at Pleshey.

The Christmas at Hemingford Grey was quiet and restful. I said Mass on Christmas Day and the Sunday afterwards only for myself and the lady warden, Miss Helen Stubbs, a delightful old lady who does wonderful work.

With all my love,

Martin.

9 June 1981

Dear Ivy,

Thank you for your letter. I'm always grateful for your support. I'm always glad to know what I should know about the matter we discussed the other day. Please never keep anything back from me that you feel I ought to know. The same applies in respect of me to you.

Thank you also for the 'message' you got while we prayed together. It was very beautiful. The copy of 'The Pain that heals' should soon be with you. Thank you also for the spiritual revelations.

With love,

Martin.

20 November 1981

Dear Ivy,

Thank you for your letter. It is good to know of your absolute support in times of adversity – though I had not previously had any doubts about it. The pain I suffered during the early period of knowledge of my imminent retirement was not entirely personal – it had important common elements too, it was, as it were, caught up into the fear and misery of many other redundant people with their sense of helplessness and hopelessness. This was the value of the experience, just as Our Lord himself came to understand the terrors that face "ordinary people" (the common people of the Gospel) during the time of his Passion, especially Gethsemane and Calvary. Your solicitude for me should be tempered with this deeper understanding, something of which I wrote in "The Pain that heals," a book that will be appreciated only by those who have suffered deeply themselves.

I doubt whether the Bishop of London would be of any help to me at the present. I shall continue with medical work until I'm shown a new way. The combination of medical and 'spiritual' seems right for me lest I lose contact with solid earth. But I am always open to a new revelation.

Thank you again for your letter and the lovely book.

With love,

Martin.

15 January 1982

Dear Ivy,

I have read your autobiographical sketch with profound humility and radiant joy. What a gift you have for expression! You could, under better life circumstances, have been a novelist of considerable stature. Thank you for sharing your life story with me in this way.

I went to Burnham Abbey on Wednesday and had a pleasant talk with Sister Mary Michael. I'm glad that all is well between us. I think she intends to write to you now.

With love,

Martin.

29 July 1985

Dear Ivy,

Yes, you have been suffering from moderate depression. This is due to your sensitivity in picking up the disturbing currents of the world generally and was sparked off by Ron's death. Bereavement in itself leads a person like you to be the basis of prolonged "accidie."

The spiritual content of your writing is excellent, so, as you say, depression is a more superficial affair. Be strong and continue in the way. I have no doubt a very strong bond unites us both. I was delighted to see you in church yesterday.

With love,

Martin.

27 July 1988

Dear Ivy,

Thank you for your letter. I am moved almost to tears by the poem and even more by all the work you have done. Our collaboration over the years has been a memorable episode in my life no less than in yours. A link has been made that will endure all adversity, and death itself will not dissolve it. You are always very much in my prayers, I hope to be off to Robertsbridge on Sunday after the Choral Eucharist. If you want to get in touch with me, just write to this address and the letter will be forwarded to me at once by the Stolls, a lovely couple that has the basement flat and the garden at the back of the building. If you want anything, be sure to ask me.

With my love,

Martin.

13 June 1989

Dear Ivy,

Thank you for your letter. Your reflections on self-esteem are indeed right. In the end, we have to accept ourselves as we are, and, in so doing, forget ourselves. Speaking personally, I find I care very much less about other people's opinions than I did even five years ago. This is a precious fruit of the ageing process. We then learn categorically that God alone is our help and all other support a very secondary matter – except, of course, on the practical level of physical help when we get ill and decrepit! I value your friendship deeply.

With my love and blessing,

Martin.

14 October 1989

Dear Ivy,

Thank you for your letter and the two beautiful poems – sheer inspiration. I hope A. gets the right spiritual help.

With love,

Martin.

I have not returned from conducting a retreat at Dunblane in Scotland.

23 October 1989

Dear Ivy,

Thank you for your latest inspirational visions: as before, they are very fine...I hope they may all be assembled into a literary unit and be widely circulated!

(The rest of the letter is destroyed by Ivy.)

28 February 1990

Dear Ivy,

Thank you for the privilege of sharing with you the wonderful insight that has been given to you. I cannot praise it highly enough. Such teaching has made your life an exceptionally valuable one for many people. I am glad we are together in eternity.

With love, blessing and prayers,

Martin.

19 November 1990

Dear Ivy,

Thank you for your letter and the beautiful writing that accompanied it. Of course, I feel betrayed by your imminent departure from London. But it is all a part of living, a groping towards eternity. We have both gained much from our time together, and the bond will certainly not be broken by mere physical separation. It will be good to feed you with the Body and Blood of Our Lord Jesus Christ, on Advent Sunday – a fitting zenith of our time together in London.

I think it better if you do not come to see me again before your departure, unless, of course, some unusual circumstances require a further meeting. We will keep in close contact by letter when you have settled down in Lincolnshire, and the prayer will not falter.

With my love,

Martin.

2 December 1990

Dear Ivy,

It was good to see you at church today. I shall be very much with you in your future life.

With my love,

Martin.

10 January 1991

Dear Ivy,

Thank you for your letter. I have noted your new address after 25 January. I enjoyed reading the enclosed spiritual writings very much.

It seems as if another world is about to embrace you as you leave for Lincolnshire. I am so glad you have had no difficulty in selling the Walthamstow house. I wonder what next Tuesday will bring the world—I can only hope that reason governs events and a major war is averted, but in the end, all things work together for good for those who love God.

I shall treasure the memory of our meetings both at Cranley Place and here – two souls in complete harmony.

I look forward to correspondence with you according to your wish.

With love,

Martin.

30 January 1991

Dear Ivy,

Thank you for your two letters, the one in front of London and the one I have just received in front of Spalding. Indeed, you have now attained freedom, and it will be your "duty and joy" to import that freedom to Geoffrey (*sic)* and Christopher, as well as those living alongside you.

With love and blessing,

Martin.

28 February 1991

Dear Ivy,

Thank you for your letter, the arrival of which has coincided so wonderfully with peace in the Gulf. I could never have hoped for such a speedy termination of hostilities. Now we must all work towards a real lasting peace in the Middle East, remembering especially Our Lord's homeland. May it yet become a focus of reconciliation between Christian, Jew and Muslims! I have been severely anguished on the psychic level by the hostilities. Now comes a time of reappraisal and rebirth coinciding with our Easier.

While I spoke (or rather wrote) about giving of yourself freely to your sons and your new friends, I simply meant that you should not retreat into yourself in defiance of your new surroundings. Continue the good work you did when you lived in London; do not be browbeaten by Agro in the community where you now live and function. The church situation seems remarkably promising for a rural town. I believe more people are coming to Christ once more. Certainly, we have had up to 70 in our own morning congregation as of late. It will be fascinating to see whether the numbers hold up now that the Gulf war is over. War does make more people more religious!

I, myself, am very well. The Retreat programme has now spread. I did a midweek retreat at Woking last week and the atmosphere was lovely. Next week I'm at a catholic house in Sayers Common (Hassocks) a Monday to Thursday retreat. I shall be interested to see how this fares. The Eucharist is a sad stumbling block, but no doubt its divisive nature can be breached by loving-kindness.

I am glad Jeffrey and Christopher are well in their work. It is wonderful that you three are now as close together in a situation and well as love.

It seems that my church has been given a reprieve of five years, but when I have it is more debatable, that it will be allowed a priest for itself. I am not writing any books at present, but the various articles I am called on to contribute are quite enough to be going on with!

With my love and constant prayer,

Martin.

26 March 1991

Dear Ivy,

Thank you for your two letters, the lovely Easter card and the equally lovely poem. I myself am very busy, this week, but hope to get away into the country next week.

With love and ceaseless prayer,

Martin.

1 May 1991

Dear Ivy,

Thank you so much for your letter and the birthday card. In fact, I spent April 30 at Pleshey conducting a retreat. It was a good occasion but the weather was cold and some of the retreatants were disturbed. I was pleased to return here yesterday. I had quite a severe depression in the months of Lent – occasioned to some extent by the Gulf crisis – but now, thank God, I feel much better. I am glad things are going well with you, and am delighted to receive your writings. Yes, contemplative prayer has indeed finally returned for both of us.

I too believe that your dear mother has come to a full reconciliation with you. It takes a long time (However we consider time in the life beyond death) for many souls to be able to receive the full love of God. He loves, but we are so indrawn. This is the burden of free will. I am now also fully reconciled to my mother and father-what a wonderful experience it is to be at peace with one's loved ones. This, in the end, will be everybody, but at present family, relationships are crucial in our spiritual development.

Christopher came well through that travail. I suspect there is a "familial" element in gallstones, at least on some occasions. To have had to have the gallstones removed at the age of only 26 is certainly unusual enough to suggest that in your case a hereditary element did play its part. At any rate, Christopher is older than you were – but gall bladder trouble is much less frequent in men than in women.

1 never cease to thank you for our deep friendship. May it continue here for many years! In eternity, it is well preserved.

With love,

Martin.

7 June 1991

Dear Ivy,

Thank you for your last letter. I'm so busy with various retreats and conferences that I have barely time for lengthy correspondence.

I am glad to say that the depression lifted – I suspect it was a "picking up" of the nasty general atmosphere at the time of the Gulf crisis.

I have little otherwise to say. It is obvious that our contact is bound to cease at a physical level now that you live in the country, but I never forget you in my prayers. Our association was ever long and faithful but like everything else in life, it has to be tested as we make our way in life, prayer is the essential link.

With love and blessings,

Martin.

20 September 1991

Dear Ivy,

I was delighted to receive your card remembering my date of ordination tomorrow. I'm, as I wrote in my last letter, pretty busy with counselling and healing work in the flat, retreat conducting and looking after the church. I had a nice holiday during most of August in the country and came back to London in a much more relaxed state.

I am not writing any books at present, but have my hands full with (my) articles for the vicar's magazine. My health is good, thank God.

I hope all goes well with you in your new abode. If anything goes amiss, do let me know. I pray for you each morning.

With love and blessing,

Martin.

I'm to speak at Lincoln in a healing centre on Saturday 19 October (St Luke's tide). It will be interesting to see how it goes. I'm to stay with a doctor in Grantham. The bishop himself asked me to come.

5 February 1992

Dear Ivy,

Thank you for your letter. Yes, a review of the past gives us great insight into the present with the hope of amending the future. You were quite right in being disturbed by my brusque May letter, but its tone was not fortuitous.

In 1982, when I was declared redundant from the Royal College of Surgeon, I had to make an agonising choice of doing pathology in a general hospital or quitting the profession and spending my time seeing people here (I mention this right at the end of "The Quest for Wholeness"). I decided on the latter course out of compassion for the people who came here for counselling and healing. Had it been a full-time hospital pathologist, all this work would have had to be discontinued. You are one of those whose situation made my choice for me. I do not regret it, as I say, in the book. It was clearly what God wanted me to do.

When the time came for you to leave London, I said I suppose you cannot come here anymore. It was your reply that hurt. Tossing your head, a characteristic gesture of yours, you said that, of course, you would stop coming to see me, just like that. There was no indication of regret at all, and whatever you may say now, I know this is true. You attended the Advent Mass, and that was that.

Please do not misunderstand me. I did not criticise your move from London. Indeed, I applaud it for the obvious reasons for getting out of a squalid area of London and living in the fresh countryside. I was more or less an object in your spiritual journey.

When you did arrive at Spalding, you seemed to see that you had been too thoughtless and suggested that we carry on a correspondence. But the belated nature of this offer as well as your attempts to enter my private life in respect of depression, I then had made it clear to me that this correspondence should end at once – apart from the time factor.

I am glad that the September letter was back to 'normal', as I hope it will continue to be now that the air is cleared. We may certainly correspond in the future according to what I can do to be of help to you. I still pray for DT's mother. And of course for you.

With my love,

Martin.

17 February 1992

Dear Ivy,

Thank you for your letter. I would not have written to you had you not asked about my May re(treat) to-do. Speaking the truth in love seemed right to me, even if, apparently, I got it all wrong. So let it be. We both have work to do, and I hope God preserves us for some time yet. I am glad to have been of service to you in your spiritual writings during our many years of cooperation.

With my love,

Martin.

8 April 1992

Dear Ivy,

Thank you for your letter. I am free for the morning up to about 10.30 am when I go to church to say Mass at 11.45 am. You could come to see me here before I leave or else we could meet in church before the Mass and spend some time there afterwards. I am engaged in the afternoon.

It would indeed be good to see you again after nearly two years – as it will be by then. Thank you also for your recent letter about St Joseph. I was extremely moved by its contents, as it seemed to contain a very helpful message for me – rather different than I would think from that due to D and A. But who knows?

With my love,

Martin.

14 June 1992

Dear Ivy,

Thank you for your letter. It appears to me that you should try to trace your sister to seek a meeting. How you set about doing this I do not know, but the indication is that you will not be at peace until you at least make a direct effort at a meeting/reconciliation with her. Maybe she seeks your help either here or on the other side of life. Keep her and your mother daily in your prayers, and also your father. No doubt, you already pray for all three of them.

Thank you for the lovely poem. It will be good to meet soon.

With love and constant prayer,

Martin.

20 July 1992

Dear Ivy,

Thank you for the letter and the inspired communication that has come to you. Forgiveness and love are the obverse sides of the same coin. Neither need be associated with any emotion, but they usually are, of course. I look forward to our meeting in October (1st). I am due to go to Robertsbridge for my August break at the end of the week – after the Choral Eucharist at Holy Trinity.

With my love,

Martin.

22 September 1992

Dear Ivy,

This is just a short note to thank you for your letter, the lovely poem and the fine card commemorating my 17 years of ordination to the priesthood. How time flies!

I shall look forward to seeing you at about 11 am on Thursday 1 October, nine days' time.

With my love,

Martin.

28 November 1992

Dear Ivy,

You were given about the Resurrection gardens. How beautiful, how full of grace! My book, "Life Eternal" is due to be published next May-June. I expect to receive the page proofs at Christmas time. I too shall look with interest to D's future career. The Bishop of London visited my church on Thursday 26 and seemed to be very impressed with its beauty. He is obviously a good man – what more can one say about anyone?

With my love,

Martin.

As usual, I am busy, but retreats are over until the end of January.

2 February 1993

Dear Ivy,

Thank you for your letter. Unfortunately, the period 22–24 April will coincide with a time that I am out of London (after the midday Eucharist on 22nd, which is a Thursday), so perhaps you can suggest another time. Sunday afternoon, 25 April would be good for me. I'm to do a priests' retreat at Hemingford Grey from 26 to 30 April. It is lovely that you have an Easter birthday for your 75 anniversary.

With my love,

Martin.

1 April

Dear Ivy,

Thank you for your letter. Yes, it would be good to see you here at 3.15 pm on Sunday, 25 April.

With my love,

Martin.

30 April 1993

Dear Ivy,

Thank you for your letter and the birthday card. No, I would not consider coming down to Holbeach to preach at a Sunday service; my own church needs me more in the morning and I have other duties in the afternoon. By 'a professional capacity'. I meant a major event in the area, say a Saturday meeting organised by the bishop (as happened last year in Grantham). I am getting too old to disperse my gifts profligately to all and sundry. Indeed, I'm doing far too much work at present with regard to retreats and quiet days. I know it is wise to cut down activities while one is still reasonably well, otherwise a major breakdown can all too easily occur, as it did in 1984, a time I shall never forget.

I was very sorry to hear of your visual impairment. I missed not being with you last Sunday, but we must hope for a future meeting.

With my love,

Martin.

18 May 1993

Dear Ivy,

Thank you for your letter and beautiful poem that well deserves to be published. It brings the Gospel down to earth very appropriately.

With my love,

Martin.

10 July 1993

Dear Ivy,

Thank you for your letter. I am sorry to learn of the deterioration in your sight, of course, it will be all right for your friend to accompany you to the flat. I am also sorry to hear about Jeffrey's accident. What a nasty series of misfortunes have followed your son and you. I hope Christopher at least is well.

With all blessings and love,

Martin.

3 August 1993 (postmark)

Dear Ivy,

I have read your profound meditation while you were on retreat with great interest. You certainly reached the heart of existence in this glimpse of reality. Your work on earth has been a great blessing to many.

I am glad to have played a part in your work. I'm at present on holiday in East Sussex (until 18 August), but my mail is redirected here from London.

With my love,

Martin.

19 November 1993

Dear Ivy,

Thank you for your letter and the moving meditation on the wood of the cross. I'm sorry that your sight has deteriorated so much, but am glad you can see to read and write. I myself am as active as ever. My year's retreats are now over. The next one, at Woking, is due to be conducted in February next year. The deliverance work goes on steadily. I am sure my friend is helping me "on the other side of death," but I still await someone who may be able to help at this side of the transition. Maybe no one will turn up. I certainly feel better than when we met two months ago (on 14 September, to be precise), but the loss still hurts me as a bereavement should. "Life Eternal" is, I believe, selling well, and the reviews in the "Church Times" and "Methodist Recorder" have been favourable. A few friends have not been able to understand the basis of the book, but, on the whole, most of them like it very much.

I am awaiting the furore in the London Diocese when the first women deacons are preordained to the priesthood. I would not like to be in those women's shoes then, so London parishes, poor things!

Keep cheerful as the cold winter embraces us all.

With my love,

Martin.

29 November 1993

Dear Ivy,

Thank you for your loving letter – so full of wisdom! The "loss" of my friend means something more than the usual bereavement situation; I lack someone to protect me in my deliverance work. So far no one has turned up who can help me as she did, but I feel, as you do, that God knows all about it. Meanwhile, the work goes on full steam ahead. Thank you for your support on early Friday morning. It is good to have a loyal friend at hand (I have noted the changed telephone number starting on 16 December.)

As real as a prayer for the dead, if you read pages 109 and 110 sequentially, I'm here discussing the Evangelical views of heaven and feel at the end of a single life, when prayer is unnecessary, as I explain at the top of page 110. In fact, Conservative Evangelicals are rising to pray for the dead. I'm surprised this section evoked any query from you since the implications are obvious. You and I do not subscribe to Conservative Evangelicalism, so we have direct access to prayer for the dead, thank God! I hope you may elucidate this matter to your mind.

With my love,

Martin.

2 December 1993

Dear Ivy,

Thank you for your letter. What you write about the work ahead for me is absolutely true. I had suspected this already, but your confirmation is of great blessing to me. I too hope we may meet again sometime next year.

With love and constant prayer,

Martin.

3 February 1994

Dear Ivy,

Thank you for your letter. I can see you here at 2 pm on Saturday, 9 July. Please confirm this. My health is, thank God, very good at present, but your dream may be premonitory, warning me to take care. Let us pray I remain in good health to do the work ahead of me.

With my love,

Martin.

2 March 1994

Dear Ivy,

Thank you for your lovely letter. I am at present conducting a retreat at The Abbey House, Glastonbury, which is due to end on the 4th. So far it is going very well, praise be to God! Your experience of God showing you the correctness of women priests is most moving, as well as spiritually evidential. By all means, ask Desmond to pray for me. I felt very much better the morning after I telephoned you, and this has continued, though the retreat has been taxing spiritually.

I do have a special ministry, but, praise be to God, I am sustained by his grace and my friends on earth, none of whom I value more than you for your spiritual insight.

With my love,

Martin.

7 April 1994

Dear Ivy,

Thank you for your lovely poem. I'm on holiday in East Sussex after the Easter Eucharist and hope to return to London on the 9th in two days' time. It is wonderful to get out of London even for six days.

With my love,

Martin.

4 May 1994

Dear Ivy,

Thank you for your birthday card, letter and script. The last is most interesting and may well be a presage of your transition to life beyond death. Your inspiration has not wavered. I enclose a copy of "Dark Victory."

With my love,

Martin.

21 July 1994

Dear Ivy,

Thank you for your message. It indeed does speak to my condition, reminding me of the immanent divine presence even when one feels lonely and isolated. May your work progress well.

With my love,

Martin.

1 October 1994

Dear Ivy,

Thank you for your letter and the card remembering my date of ordination to the priesthood. I can see you here at 3 pm on Saturday, 3 December; please confirm this.

With my love,

Martin.

10 December 1994

Thank you for your letter. I'm glad Desmond liked my Church Newsletter article. It clearly has done quite a lot of good, praise be to God.

As regards my bedroom, there was no motive other than to show you where I slept and prayed quite a lot. As you said, it was simple. I have not been involved directly with witch doctors; I wonder how you gained this misconception. I suppose I might have been peripherally in contact when I served in the Army in Nigeria as a part of my National Service some 40–50 years ago. How time flies! I also had no 'aya'. The nurses I had were white women, at least in my infancy and early childhood, and there was no mention by them of the occult. Demonic forces, such as I deal with in my deliverance ministry, are not mediated by witch doctors, at least in my work, unless I minister to West Africans.

I mention all this simply to put your mind at rest. It is so easy to put two and two together to get five or even six! Thank you for your meditation on Gethsemane.

With my love,

Martin.

(Ivy writes back on 15 December because Martin's letter directly contradicts a conversation Martin had with Ivy about being attacked by Peruvian witch doctors on 25 February. Also, long before she left London, she asserts that he did refer to his 'aya' whom Ivy assumed was black. At the end of the copy of her reply to him, she writes for her own benefit:

(It is very fortunate that I do record most of M.I. s letters and phone calls as I should begin to wonder about myself. He is a difficult man. Not having given me carte blanche more than once, I feel free to do this.)

2 January 1995

Dear Ivy,

Thank you for your lovely visionary poem. I'm well but fearfully overworked. Praise God, I have completed my book about Angels! It has to be handed into SPCK by the end of January.

With my love,

Martin.

20 September 1995

Dear Ivy,

Thank you for your letter. Yes, I shall have been priested 20 years tomorrow and members of my congregation are giving me a little luncheon in the vestry hall after the Sunday morning service. I am thrilled to learn of the miraculous improvement in the sight. One can only say, "Praised be God!"

A new book of mine entitled "Angels: Messengers of Light" is due to be published by SPCK on October 12. There will be an article about it in the Daily Mail at about the same time, I especially will be interviewed and photographed.

Needless to say, I eschew all publicity, but the publishers hope that the publicity will give the sales a boost! I am also giving a lecture on the subject on October 19 and I am enclosing a leaflet for your amusement. Needless to say, I would not expect you to conic down to London from 6.30 pm to 8.00 pm to hear me speak'

With much love,

Martin.

26 September 1996

Dear Ivy,

What a joy it is to hear once more from you: a most Christian saint! No, I have not recovered in the slightest from my crippledom, despite various fruitless treatments, and I am falling all over the place, hurting especially my right knee and my skull. Today I am to visit a podiatrist, a doctor who specialises in foot problems and shoes.

I suppose that my time of 'moving onwards' is drawing near at hand. I am 69 now and will be surprised if I make the biblical three score and ten years. I shall not be sorry to 'shuffle off this mortal coil', as Shakespeare puts it in 'Hamlet'. I have written two final books: one on "exorcism" and the other on "doubt." The former has been hailed enthusiastically by SPCK, while the latter has been commissioned by Cassell's. The publishers have not seen the draft yet.

Do keep in touch.

With my love,

Martin.

I have been dismissed from my church because of my infirmity. The congregation has been so very bitter about the way I have been treated. "Father, forgive them for they know not what they do."

9 October 1994

Dear Ivy,

Thank you for your letter. I could see you here on Saturday, November 16 at 3.30 pm. Please confirm this appointment. I am feeling better than previously.

With my love and prayers,

Martin.

29 April 1998

Dear Ivy,

Thank you for your letter and birthday card. I think the three poems are all equally beautiful. It is a pity that a collection of your poems cannot be printed. I am glad DT is rid of his curate, and pray with you that he may have some joy now. He deserves it.

With my love,

Martin.

29 May 1998

Dear Ivy,

Thank you for your letter. I am sure it was no coincidence that I was reminiscing about Rosslyn with a mutual friend only yesterday over the telephone. I knew of her MS and am glad she is still able to function in the first marriage I conducted.

I am steadily improving in my walking and can walk in Battersea Park now – the distance to and from my home must be nearly a mile. The Parkinson's disease is under good medical control. Yes, I have the God-given qualities of endurance and courage. I hope you are well.

With love, blessing and prayer,

Martin.

20 July 1998

Dear Ivy,

Thank you for your beautiful letter about your arrival at Langthorne, distressing and so noble. I came to England in June 1951 with my parents from South Africa. We all enjoyed a tour of Western Europe before finally arriving in London towards the end of July. They spent about a month here before returning to Johannesburg, having first settled me in a guesthouse in Bayswater. I did a course of study at Hammersmith Hospital from the end of September to the following January and then passed the exam to become a member of the Royal College of Physicians in March 1952. A month later, I was appointed House Physician to the Professorial Unit. This lasted about six months and then I could get no job in clinical medicine. The professor previously suggested my becoming a pathologist but in the interim, I looked for a local appointment in general medicine – one immediately on offer was at Langthorne and I took it.

Like you, I found it very depressing. 1t was at the time a pioneer geriatric hospital and only a minority of its patients ever left its premises. But I liked the other junior doctors working there. We were all 'riff-raff' by English standards. I, a South African, an Irish doctor couple, an Irish widow and a Czechoslovak, immediately come to mind. At any rate, my contract came to an end four months later in March 1953 and I followed the career of pathology in Wolverhampton until 1955, when I was called up to do two years' National Service as a pathologist. During all this while, I was drawing closer to unusual people with spiritual interests; God was slowly drawing me into Christian service as an Anglican priest. What a slog, but what wonderful people I have met on the way, not the least you yourself!

With love,

Martin.

8 August 1998

Dear Ivy,

Thank you for your fine letter and also the parish magazine. I did enjoy the vicar's letter. It struck two chords: Judaism in relation to Christianity and also Robert Llewellyn's recently published autobiography "Memories and

Reflections" in which I receive praise for my psychic and spiritual work. He is clearly a delightful man. I am glad you have him as your priest. Please give him my regards.

The moving account of your thoughts about the disposal of your mortal remains has made a deep impression on me. It reminds me of the treasured hours we had together in London before you moved to Holbeach. We were meant for one another, and I do not doubt that we will be in close contact in the greater life ahead of us. I would be honoured to receive a copy of your wonderful meditation. But please do not over-tire yourself in doing this. Your description of the River Nene emptying into the Wash fills my mind with sweet images. East Anglia and Lincolnshire somehow have a sterner countenance than the counties of the west, and they are colder too in the winter months. Yes, I would not mind being with you near the Wash on the banks of the Nene.

I am walking much better, thank God. I am making great strides, both in my gait and my progress. And at last, summer has broken through! Let us hope for mild, mellow autumn to compensate for the disappointing May, June and July.

With my love,

Martin.

18 August 1998

Dear Ivy,

Thank you for sharing your luminous meditation with me. The eternal infant reflects the glory of Jesus on the way to Calvary. The sea that recedes from the Mother and her Son is a symbol of all that is evil and corrupt in the world. At times, the evil seems to be overwhelming, but He is always at our side. This eternal presence can be actualised in our life as we hear in the depth of our soul, 'Come, follow me.'

When I descended into hell last year dining the five weeks period of semi-consciousness, my rational mind lay shattered with total amnesia, but my spiritual mind was extremely active; it was in complete darkness in which I could 'sense' a vast concourse of isolated souls, quite unable to communicate with any others. The desolation was terrifying, and yet I remember so well how lacking in fear I was. When I recovered, this absence of fear in the face of a terrifying situation struck me as strange as well as memorable. The answer suddenly came to me later on: I was surrounded by the love of God. You have experienced the same truth from a different angle. I know that God's love (grace) is not contingent on our worthiness, but until we move from self-centredness to universal concern, we cannot be open to God's love. The souls I saw in my period of semi-consciousness were a selection of those who had once lived typically selfish lives on earth. But as soon as they can see the light and repent, they will hear 'Come'. I believe that those like us when we die will help our backsliding brethren to the light, for heaven cannot be complete until we all are included.

Thank you for the nice Lincolnshire postcard. The poem is beautiful.

With my love,

Martin.

4 September 1998

Dear Ivy,

Thank you for sending me your very evocative dream. It seems to fit in with Isaiah 43. This chapter comprises mostly a rhapsody of God's unconditional love to his people of Israel but from verse 22 to the end, there is a different tone. They are scolded for their ingratitude and reminded of the consequences of their past sinfulness. The congregation of the church in your dream is just like this: they do nothing but expect everything. I am one with them but also apart from them, being the priest who is to give them healing. They cannot provide anything; the key is from God, and when the door of the church is opened, the Holy Spirit enters in a tremendous rush. This has, in fact, been my work as a priest (not always appreciated by the clergy who feel threatened and are envious). The voice on the phone was of God (as in Isaiah 43) and the corruption he declared was associated with the people in the church. They are unfortunately representative of most Christians (to say nothing of the majority who have no concern with God or anyone other than their own). People like you and me are rare exceptions, and we suffer for it, as I did last year. But we are close to Christ who died that others might have life. When one considers the history of the Church, one just wonders. But God's work will never be halted, thanks to people like us.

With my love and blessing,

Martin.

21 September 1998

Dear Ivy,

How lovely it is to hear from you on the twenty-third anniversary of my ordination. Our twenty-three years of friendship have proved a blessing. In joy, I remember our visits. I am also happy that you have put down new roots in Holbeach. Your poem about the advent of death is a long paean of joyful expectation. I personally can scarcely wait to go, but I know there is still work for me in this incarnation.

Thank you for the ordination card. I continue to walk better. I hope you are well too.

With my love and prayer,

Martin.

8 October 1998

Dear Ivy,

Thank you for your letter. The gates of the workhouse are a symbol of the pain that a virtuous child (and adult) has to open (understand) in their experience of incarnation. You were long forgiven; we two could never have come together so quickly and so lovingly had we not been essentially chaste.

Please give Rosslyn my love when you are on retreat at Hemmingford Grey next month. It is wonderful to know people like you, her and Tony.

With my love,

Martin.

8 November 1998

Dear Ivy,

We two could never have come together so quickly and so lovingly had we not been essentially chaste. It is wonderful to know people like you.

With my love,

Martin.

29 January 1999

Dear Ivy,

Thank you for your joyful letter. I am so pleased that my friend looks so well and conducted the retreat so excellently. Out of suffering, many good things will occur, provided we face the future with courage and faith. You, she, and I are all testimonies to this abiding truth in our own way. If life has given me none else, knowing you and Rosslyn would be sufficient.

The curate is clearly a great soul, a true mystic. I too consider myself a mystical liberal Catholic. I am glad he is directed spiritually by a Mirfield father.

My own health continues to improve, praise be to God. Obviously, the cold, wet weather cuts down the amount of walking I can do at present, but the strength in my legs is increasing. I hope to spend another two weeks in Barbados in the latter part of February, once more with my carer and his friend. "Happiness that lasts" is due to be published in March, and I shall see that a copy is sent to you. May God bless you and keep you.

With my love,

Martin.

21 April 1999

Dear Ivy,

Thank you for your letter. Please give Christopher my love when you attend the 25th anniversary of his priesthood. He has beaten me by a year!

Your attitude to a certain priest and the Danish girl who died so very young is, I am assured, the right one and admirably expressed in the letter you wrote to him. I am sure there is no need to mourn for the woman. He, like you so long ago, must leave the matter in God's hands and move on.

With my love and prayer,

Martin.

14 November 1999

Dear Ivy,

Thank you for your letter and the exquisite poem about meditation and about the river. It is a compelling symbol of endless life, fresh each day and then moving noiselessly into the cold dark might.

I hope to spend a month in New Zealand (14 December to 14 January) in the company of my two carers. Hopefully, I shall be able to avoid the cold and darkness in England for the worst of the winter – though February is pretty miserable too.

My health is somewhat better, and I can walk a little more easily. I thank God for this.

With my love,

Martin.

8 March 2001

Dear Ivy,

Thank you for your letter. I am delighted you received my book. I think the story of my life has been an exciting one, not without its loneliness and moments of depression, but never far from creativity. The present book is my twenty-third.

I am glad your health remains good. I shall be 74 on the very last day of April. Yes, life has been a very long journey, but every minute of it has been worthwhile. I feel more at peace than ever before. The three poems are beautiful.

With my love,

Martin.

28 September 2001

Dear Ivy,

Thank you for your most interesting letter and the lovely poem, 'A Wounded World' at the end. Oddly enough, I too have written a poem on this theme. I have called it 'An Act of Barbarity 11 September'. It consists of seven flowing sonnets.

With my love and prayers,

Martin.

25 October 2001

Dear Ivy,

I thank you for your latest letter. The experience of intercession you had during the Sunday morning service was indeed profound and extremely moving. First, I dominated the scene and then Rosslyn Miller appeared as well in increasing strength so that she and I eventually seemed and indeed were, as one. All else seemed lost in holding us there. It is amazing that as you walked to the Altar rail, there was nothing else other than us three. The impression was so overwhelming that you were almost too overcome to drink from the chalice. Later in the afternoon, when you considered the matter at a greater distance, you knew that it had indeed been (although) it was as though it had not been.

I have no doubt that your interpretation was right: two quite different priests whom you care greatly about, both suffering from incapacitating diseases of the nervous system but nevertheless, carrying on God's work with devotion to the community. It is a painful privilege to do this work, but if one carries on regardless, one grows in love with many people. This is the kernel of spiritual life. Our pain is the world's gain, compared with which our weakness is our greatest joy. We are all here to serve our fellows, but only a few of us understand this.

With my love,

Martin.

26 February 2002

Dear Ivy,

Thank you for your letter. I thought the poem was beautiful. I am, on the last lap of my Barbados holiday and due to return to London on 1 March. My own poems were rejected by three publishers, but a close friend has urged me to keep them for future use, so I have not discarded them.

With my love,

Martin.

15 June 2002

Dear Ivy,

Thank you for your letter and the lovely piece of poetry a beautiful tribute to sleep, which embraces us in healing oblivion between the sufferings of the day's hours of disturbance and worry. There was someone with me when you telephoned me. It was this occasion that made me appear tired, for I could not afford you my full attention.

I remember the days when you lived in London and you regularly visited me, and how sad I felt when you moved away to Lincolnshire.

With my love and prayers,

Martin.

21 September 2004

Dear Ivy,

Thank you for your letter and the lovely picture card. I am greatly incapacitated, living largely in a wheelchair as you know, but my spirit is joyful as I remember my time at Holy Trinity Prince Consort Road. I am delighted that you also are flourishing in your own home despite your severely ill health.

Prayer is the essential action, an opening of the soul to God.
With my love,

Martin.

Just one more fragment of a letter remains, the rest destroyed by Ivy, but this was something she needed to keep. Date unknown. It says in Martin's handwriting:

I think of you with great love for what you are in our God.

Ivy found this too precious to destroy. It was left to be found, and here it is. It expresses Martin's understanding of his relationship with Ivy in precisely the terms in which Ivy in her Spiritual Diary describes her relationship with him. We should read their disagreements, perhaps as quarrels of 'lovers in the Lord—'

The letters that Ivy kept and did not destroy end here.

One of the issues which Ivy raises from time to time during their meetings in London is the matter of homosexuality. She never reveals what he replies to her but there was one occasion in August 1989 when Martin was conducting a retreat at The Royal Foundation of St Katharine, Stepney when out of the blue she reports him making the following remarks, describing them as his views as a doctor. She does add, "Why, I wonder, did he do this?"

He says, "Homosexuality is not normal, but it is not evil, it is a psycho-pathological area condition and celibacy should be the ultimate aim." However, on 8 December 1994, Ivy writes in her spiritual diary: "Received from M.I. yesterday the promised Holy Trinity newsletter. The article he has written on homosexuality called 'Tolerance and Toleration' is excellent. He, like me, has come a very long way on this subject and I am so pleased that a man of his standing has seen fit to write it."

We know that Martin remained unmarried all his life and described himself to Ivy as coming to true celibacy but nowhere is there any direct indication of his sexual orientation. However, in old age, when he could no longer look after himself, he decided that he needed to find a living in carer. In the event, he found two living in carers, two young New Zealand men, a qualified nurse and his 'friend', who looked after him for the remainder of his life. He even went with them on holiday to Barbados and visited their families in New Zealand. These two carers were not celibate, they were a gay couple. Martin died on 23 October 2007, cared for by them. "He died in their arms."

Throughout their friendship, the issue, above all, which drew Martin to Ivy, was her visionary experience. It was in this developing awareness within her experience of God's grace that hers was a particular vocation to be given these 'visions' that Martin found both fascinating and personally beneficial to himself, as well as potentially important to a wider public. Because of this, he encouraged her to accept that they should be published after her death. In order to fulfil this intention, we now move on in the following chapters to examine some of these visions, beginning with the first hesitant steps and going forward to some of her mature experiences. Not everything could be included in this first book. Plenty of material remains for subsequent publication in due course.

Chapter 3
First Steps

Ivy Goodley's spiritual journey was marked by two sayings. One was given to her at West Malling Abbey while in retreat. She went to the abbey for her first private retreat on 27 July – 2 August 1974. She told me that while she was standing beside the stream that gently meanders through the abbey grounds, pondering in prayer what God was calling her to be and to do, the words came to her "Lead gently by the still waters of love." These remained with her throughout her journey and the last vision of water that she recorded on 14 and 19 November 2005 (see Chapter 6) was a cosmic vision of "the waters of love" rising up and destroying the power of darkness. This is why the title of this book is "Waters of Love." However, reading her spiritual diary for evidence of this moment during that private retreat, there is no mention of it and I thought that I would have to rely on her conversation with me, sometime later, as evidence that this is what happened. However, in her spiritual diary on 19 September 1989, while in retreat at West Malling, she writes the following:

"I sit and write in this familiar little room, I first came here in July 1974, much water (spiritual water) under the bridge since then, the words return as I know they would, 'Lead gently by the still waters of love.', these words have meant so much over the years, constantly teaching and re-teaching."

Here is the evidence needed to affirm the significance of that moment fifteen years before when she made her first visit to the abbey.

The second saying is first recorded in her spiritual diary on 2 September 1975. She writes, "I rather like this from T.S.Eliot: 'And all shall be well, all manner of thing shall be well, by the purification of the motive in the ground of our beseeching'." She is apparently unaware at this stage that Eliot is quoting Julian of Norwich, although in due course she does discover this. This saying flows through her writings like the first saying and is included in the last thing that she wrote in her spiritual diary on 21 October 2008 (see Chapter 6).

This chapter sets out the first few experiences of Ivy, which come to her as a complete surprise. These 'visions' begin over 30 years of experience to come. At first, she is not sure how to cope with what is happening to her but reasonably quickly, as she discovers more and more about the experiences she has, she begins to evaluate them on the one hand while on the other hand recognising that these 'visions' are given to her without any effort on her part and emerge often very slowly over weeks and months as her capacity to receive what she by now believes God is sending to her.

Because of the long periods involved in these 'visions' (unlike some other mystics such as Julian of Norwich who received her 'visions' in a very short space of time and then spent many years pondering them before she put pen to paper) I have found it necessary here and throughout this book to set out in Ivy's own words the diary entries which describe them. Often they are written in the context of written material about family issues, visits she makes, people she meets etc and sometimes, but not always, it is necessary to include these to put the 'visions' in their proper context.

From Ivy Goodley's Spiritual Diary

1976

2 January

A lovely talk this morning with Mrs Harrison, sharing and at Mass recalled the words "Lead gently by the still waters of love."...I wonder where or why on occasion, I am so aware of this water, although even that is changing now in as much as there is no struggle on my part, the water swirls around, but I am carried easily along and I am not afraid...whatever I experience from time to time in the way of doubt, instability almost in that I am unsure, it seems to be contradicting because still the 'core' is intact and at peace, surface struggles, but they can be painful.

23 January

The water seems to be broadening out, widening, it seems to be incorporated in vastness as to sky, and yet it doesn't seem to be the sea…limitless, on and on, not boisterous, yet not still…it fills one…stillness. Even to say the Lord's Prayer becomes difficult. I often find that it has gone completely…with all these contacts with people, and even in spiritual friendships, quite often I experience inner loneliness, other people tend to recede, even those one loves.

(Note this very early reference to aloneness and loneliness. See Chapter 4)

26 January

A mixed day, long periods of deep prayer, the water intruded into everything, at first this morning it was vast, and a great expanse of the sky seemed intermingled with it, suddenly – literally – I realised it was not confined anymore but above ground and immense. Later today, it was back but as a waterfall. I seemed to be outside of myself looking at it, it fell down and was carried swiftly away into the vast expanse, after what seemed to me to be a considerable time I found myself looking for the source – upwards – to high rocks and crags, but I could see nothing from where it was coming, it fell like a sheet, crystal clear…Other than this has been very difficult, all sorts of things presented themselves in my mind, reasons for letting go.

14 February

In-depth today the water was vast – on and on – the air, black clouds appeared, and the water below was equally rough, then light and the water was calm, this happened several times, the clouds were darker and darker, the sea was fierce and rather frightening, but eventually all was calm and still. I thought or was it just there in my mind – that from the water the spirit soars upwards, unless one is becalmed in water in which case one does not move but stays in tranquillity and peace, but if the water is moving although very slowly, one is carried along and eventually there is land, but in the air above the clouds is eternity, freedom, no beginning, no end, neither at this point does there seem to be any wind, rather all is motionless, after this blankness…from the air all is visible, water – land – from the water no land is visible, but the sky is, what does this mean? I do not know why I want to say this, but I want to say "Do not be afraid, the love of God is beyond our understanding and in him only do we achieve wholeness." I closed my eyes and there was rest.

Comment: This is Ivy Goodley's first experience of an incremental 'visionary' experience and she is finding it difficult to describe it and indeed to find any language adequate to express what is happening. A significant phrase is "I thought, or was it just there in my mind?" She is uncertain whether she is interpreting what is happening or whether the interpretation is being given to her by the grace of God. In the end, the words that come to her about the love of God will become the leitmotif of so much that is to be given to her in the future, but at this stage, she records the words unsure why they are there. However, they bring her rest.

On my advice, she has been reading St John of the Cross. She tells a senior member of the congregation that she is doing this and receives the response, "Oh no, my dear. St John of the Cross is not for the likes of you!" Fortunately, she rejects this piece of 'advice' and continues to read him. He sets out some tests for accepting or rejecting 'visionary' experiences, which are in essence, do not accept particular knowledge, only general information and reject all experience which leads to a weakening or destruction of faith, hope and love and accept only that which reinforces these three basic Christian virtues. On the basis of these two tests, she accepts the words "Do not be afraid, the love of God is beyond our understanding and in him only do we achieve wholeness" and finds rest. It is a sign that they are God-given, not from her own imagination and not from satanic temptation.

We now move on to further experience a year later, showing Ivy's growth in describing what she receives more clearly.

1977

6 May

"In my Father's house are many mansions."

The ascending of Our Lord into the Father, the return into the Father, "In my Father's house are many mansions." The mansions are contained in the house of the Father. The Son, the head pierced by the crown of thorns is a mansion, (the) seat of control for all parts of the body, the (place) of thought, the seat of the will, perhaps the word 'intellectual centre' could be used. The 'whole' body of

Christ is ' the House', the centre towards which the soul travels – the five wounds are the mansions through which we must pass before dwelling in the House, the last mansion and the most important one, and the one we shall probably be longest in – if we ever reach this mansion at all, is contained within the riven side of Christ, it is the mansion of the heart, of Divine Love, the 'room' that transcends any intellect, the 'room' of change as in 'rebirth'.

7 May

Mass this morning…"In my Father's House are many mansions" I retained this in depth, the line had returned spontaneously. And although I thought of it briefly in the context I had always thought, which really was not in much depth at all, rather perhaps as stages, we go through to reach the ultimate, I knew immediately that although it could not be discounted, it was not as I recognised it now, for it was aligned to two things, the ascension of Our Lord, the absorption into the Father and to the wounds of Our Lord. The Father's House is contained in the Son, the way to the Father is through the Son, the wounds have both physical and Spiritual content, physical as in the agony of the flesh, Spiritual as in the agony of the mind, emotions and spirit of man, the eternal search for the Father found only within the Son. The mansions we must travel through to reach the Father are contained within Our Lord, his wounds are the doors we enter through into his suffering, within him are the chambers we must pass through, the last chamber being within his riven side beneath the heart…Spiritual friendships are usually entered into through the wounds of suffering, one within the other, to be able to share pain is to share all. Spiritual friendships contain always the living presence of Our Lord, and this is the secret of their 'life'. Later the line returned 'Lead gently by the still waters of love'…"In my Father's house are many mansions," the greying figure of the dying Lord returned, "Come unto me all you that are heavy laden and I will refresh you." Mansions as places of refreshment, stops along the way, this followed from me at that point spontaneously but I do not see the mansions as being along the Spiritual road as such, but contained within Our Lord, on entering the first Mansion in the House/Christ, the first mansion being the head, the directive of the will, reason etc, but the spiritual knowledge given and received goes far beyond the reason and the will. Although they are very necessary lest we stray into a world of fantasy, I do not see love coming from reason, if we stopped to reason, then love would not progress to much depth. Divine love cannot be calculated – given out in doses – it is incalculable and flows incessantly. Nevertheless to enter into Christ through his wounds is to enter a haven, because of his acceptance of the whole of his suffering, and to enter into acceptance with him changes the face of suffering, our own suffering. One no longer fights it, but rather discovers a most soothing balm – a healing balm. One does not escape suffering, neither should one try to escape it…In depth the crucified Lord, the five wounds – the openings "into." Come into the 'house' of God. If one thinks of the word house/home, the place one returns to, the place one 'lives' in, a haven where we know and we feel we are safe, what lovelier thing is there than to 'see' Our Lord as this house! To travel forth and to return to, until we travel forth no more, but live permanently within. The mansions within him are our learning processes to the final mansion of absolute love, resting beneath the heart…to enter through his wounds is to be absorbed into, and if one looks upon his wounds as absorption into it, it is in a hitherto undiscovered meaning to me, we are absorbed into this living Christ, he ascends to the Father and is absorbed into the awareness within of the dying Christ, his wounds are hallowed…as he is hallowed being the house of God the Father, by his wounds shall you know him…

Contemplation of the dying Christ, the wounds becoming the focal point of the shrinking disintegrating body, this remained for some time, as the body dies all that (is) in Christ, all the love – the compassion – the obedience, and all else transform these wounds to beauty, that in his resurrection they flower for eternity. I remained in this depth aware of warmth…'Lord, show me thy face'…In the contemplation of the wounds they change from what the outward eye perceives to what the inward eye recognises as the path of perfection…the centre – the light burns briefly – a glow, then fades almost imperceptibly as one is aware again of intense suffering. Man's suffering contained in this figure upon the cross…In the disintegration of the body, the wounds are stark, as any wound is on a dying body, they appear longer because of the body's state, they stand out, through his wounds he opens himself to all who would enter and journey along the Spiritual road within.

'Come unto me'…unto the Father, he is the house in which the Father dwells 'In my Father's house'…The tide ebbs and flows through each mansion to the door of the final mansion resting beneath the heart, refining and purifying along the way, this final mansion is entered only by pure love, contained in the purity of intention, the sole motive being God…

139

The approach road contains many dangers, the hits and misses of false love, false piety etc, where the real intention is self, here is where we need help in the shape of truth…My outward eye is closed – my inward eye is open, perceiving the wounds are hallowed, contained in five centres of light, the light contained in his riven side. I cannot 'see' although I know it is there, I am blinded by the brilliance…the 'house' is the container of all that is pure, all that is true and all that is holy in the sight of God the Father, nobody is barred entry, all are equal in the sight of God…

There returns the greying body upon the cross, the receiving of it within oneself and the journey inwards to the centre, this is the part, that once impregnated, desires to enter the 'house' and begin the journey home, I do not see it as a definite beginning, knowledge, awareness, but as a very slow process, an absorption into by slow degrees of desire (if that is the right word) desire for God, at this point the disintegrating body and the receiving of Communion, the bread, "This is my body."

18 May

I am still…in depth, words come 'That I may follow thee more nearly, love thee more dearly' etc…everything slows down within myself and I am aware of this, unhurriedly thoughts of the crucifix, slowly the disintegrating body…The light that is Christ…the consecration, the bread, 'Take, eat'…The inward travelling towards the centre, the piercing of it, it rests…The return inwardly of the wounds of Our Lord, the detachment of the centre, it re-enters, it is absorbed into, and is fused, and it has entered into and is within the house.

19 May

Depth…'Lord, show me thy face'…very slowly within – communion, the travelling towards, the piercing of the centre…rest, an awareness after this rest, of the crucified Lord, an awareness also of the risen Lord. 'And he shall bear thee up'…so is God in man, so is man in God, the real spiritual journey begins through each mansion in the 'house' which is Christ, and the learning is concerned with Divine love…later a thought came, that in every man shall be planted a tree of hope.

21 May

Once the centre has been pierced, there is experienced rest, even one's breathing is still, almost imperceptible, one's mind is empty, undisturbed, there are no heights of emotion, rather an absorption into warmth, the centre is drawn gently but inexorably towards the wound of the house which is Christ, and is absorbed into.

22 May

At the end of the Hail Mary's an awareness of the Pieta, that even in death, the Mother still bears the child. I held this! There followed very slowly as before, the disintegration, "This is my body, do this, live this," the travelling towards, the piercing of the centre, the detachment of the centre and the travelling towards the 'house', absorption into, and there is a pure stream of running water cleansing those that enter, it runs through the mansions, culminating in the riven side of Our Lord…one rests. (Here I must say I do not feel I am in this, I am shown it only…) Life-giving water.

23 May

I began saying the Lord's Prayer, but I could not go on, there was the body and blood of Our Lord. "Take eat, this is my body" communion. I received inwardly, but it went no farther, it receded and faded almost immediately…later, again I began to pray, beginning with the Lord's Prayer, this time there was no hindrance, aware only of the crucifix before which all passed, I prayed…

24 May

In depth…immediately 'Take, eat,' this is my body…'do this'…the receiving of the body and blood of the Lord, communion, I 'feel' nothing, yet know that I have communicated, I am quiet, I am unable to express adequately myself…That which is pierced, travels immediately to the first mansion which is contained in the head of Our Lord, it is absorbed into, without is the suffering face, the eyes closing as death approaches, but although I am aware of this, the centre has pierced this, beyond and within is only light, a light illuminating the house…a thought intervened here of the door of a home being opened…every room within is ablaze with light, that welcomes home the traveller, one enters in and is refreshed…I rest.

25 May

I felt very silent and almost withdrawn as I woke this morning, a little later (before breakfast) as I closed my eyes, immediately the approach, 'This is my Body', I made my communion, realising at the same time that I received through the mouth, I never do this, but always through the hands, as I was first taught…the depth was indescribable, I can only say a 'sweetness in pain'…Lord, I am not worthy…afterwards, if I do try to realise what is happening…what I am receiving…it is not that I do not know, or do not understand, it is just that I do not feel anything approaching worthiness, and I am very quiet…later prayer…That which had been pierced travelled towards the head of Our Lord, resting within in light…the light receded and one was aware of conflict taking place within this mansion, one was not part of it, only aware of it, there were conflicts of doubt…self-will…non-acceptance…wrong reasoning…vain glory…materialistic values set against spiritual values…greed…all these things were set in darkness – sometimes the darkness lifted and a little light entered, only to be submerged…but this is the beginning of the purification and one may well remain in this room for a lifetime…set in the light nevertheless is truth, bound as always with love, they are immovable, time and again the conflictions hurl themselves against them, rebounding back into the darkness, these two things set in the light within this mansion are released not only through the process of purification but through the thirst of the centre…the desire of the centre for God its creator…at this point all faded…the full light returned and the waters flowed through…

28 May

The desire for God fills every mansion of the house, it is the seed of desire that enters the door of the mansion of the head, where all the conflictions must be overcome before the centre may leave this mansion for the second. Desire enters as a seed, the seed may be strong and flourish, reaching out as it grows towards the light, the seed may be weak and have many setbacks as it struggles, nevertheless, the seed of desire is there, and as it grows, it must perforce overcome the conflictions until it dwells permanently within the light when desire reaches a certain level of growth, its path is made easier by the release of love and truth which dwell permanently within the light of the house, desire for God the creator is present in degrees in all of us, but many never reach the door of the house, self-blindness, and many factors contribute to this.

30 May

The approach, the communion…we may possess the desire for the Creator, yet not recognise it. We are aware of a yearning – yet are unable to put a name to that for which we yearn, we may find ourselves searching for that which satisfies our inward longing, yet never find it because we do not recognise it for what it is, but the seed of desire that enters the mansion does recognise it, and will strive to attain it, though it falls back many times…yet will it rise again and again to reach the light…once the desire is impregnated by love and truth its outer clothes fall away and it knows it stands revealed to its Creator as it really is…it is in sorrow, as the wounds of the head of Christ taking in the suffering and afflictions of mankind are revealed to it in full, it has never known such sorrow, and never realised the depth of such love…Many times it has been thought that it has, but those instances were ripples compared to the knowledge it now receives…later in prayer – the outward face and the head crowned with thorns remained inwardly…later on I had something to eat and fell asleep…it was very hot…The mansions of the hands and feet of Our Lord are servant mansions. They say that it performs the deeds of love, controlled by love…this was so clear that I felt I must write it down immediately?

31 May

Prayer…as desire grows and is nurtured, it is aware only of that whom it seeks, its Creator, the seed grows and is swollen with love, and in this love is contained obedience and service, it longs to serve God in whatever way he asks, and becomes obedient unto his will, truth is never absent, else we may easily embark upon our own will, and be sincere in the thought that it is God's will.

1 June

Prayer…later the approach…communion…rest, complete silence…since the few days that these communions have been given, I note there is a little variation, at times the approach is immediate, at times it steals gently into prayer, halting it, then continuing from this point, at times following immediately after prayer, but it is sweet and lovely…As desire is fed in this mansion, it grows and becomes more and more one within the light, and of the light, until finally it is complete in its unity with its Creator and is secure…security of tenure…its only aim is to serve, and it may then leave this mansion and travel to the mansions of the hands and the feet, as I have been shown…the servant mansions the mansions of service – where, controlled by the first mansion, they are totally obedient to God's will, serving and abiding in his love…the way is clear, they live always and continuously in the present moment, living and serving in whatever is at hand…and the waters flow…

3 June

To be within the servant mansions is to be the servant of love, 'love serves'…one's motivation must be towards the Creator, nobody's need is too small, and nobody is so highly exalted that they are above the giving and receiving of love, or that they are above the need…the giving and receiving of human love is one of God's most beautiful gifts to his children but through the receiving and giving of Divine love we are so strengthened and warmed by him that it adds to and enhances all human love. It is a very necessary ingredient for the fulfilment, enabling a blossoming to take place where before there has been just stunted growth. The love contained within the mansions of service is only of a Divine order, no human frailty intrudes here, and it contains the pure essence of the Trinity, Father, Son and Holy Spirit.

5 June

Prayer…I 'saw' within – Our Lord upon the cross – it faded, leaving only the extended arms, taut…the approach. Communion…the pierced centre travels to the hand, the left wounded hand, through which it is absorbed 'into'…I was aware this took place, afterwards, my reasoning thought returned to the first mansion of the 'house', the centre, when ready by a desire for service – carrying it to the next mansions of the wounded hands, through the inward waters running through the 'house'…the direct absorption I 'saw' this morning?

7 June

Prayer…the centre travelling to the first mansion, is 'embedded' in at each communion thereafter. The centre, when pierced, travels to the mansion it has reached, a constant renewal, thus to the left wounded hand, is absorbed 'into' serve in love, the left I see as being of the heart. The acts of service in this mansion are spurred by love and desire for the Creator, the service alternating with long periods of passive 'being'…

144

8 June

The centre within the mansions of service is happy, it serves with joy, it is constantly receiving and constantly giving out, there is a sense of well-being, its periods of passivities are quite beautiful, it rests, it worships, it dwells 'in', it is renewed, and it becomes aware of the enclosure not as 'in' as 'enclosing', warming…The time in these mansions is controlled entirely by Divine Will and only by this may it be led to the last mansion within the house.

9–11 June

During silent prayer, there was immediately within me the mansion of the riven side of Christ, the last mansion…words flowed into me, Sacred wound, beneath the heart (Next day) at Communion my thoughts return to the riven side of Christ, wherein is housed love, and from which it flows. The last mansion is the 'house' of God the Father…I meditated a little on the riven side of Christ, absorption into this mansion of the house of God, wherein is contained the Trinity, Father, Son and Holy Spirit…the heart centre containing love and purity…Later in prayer, the absorption into the wounded side of Christ is an absorption into pure love, the mansion housing the Holy Trinity…the pulse…the Divine pulse, the impregnated soul entering here is entirely at rest, and it has found that which it sought. The heartbeat is neither fast nor slow, it is even, never changing…The soul loves, it worships, it is utterly devoted and obedient. The next morning at Mass, I asked at the altar for love, that I may give it…In prayer, the pierced centre travelling towards the riven side, the absorption into…no dark thing may enter here, the Trinity is housed in light, the soul dwells in the light of the Father, Son and Holy Spirit…it is the mansion of pure delight. Nevertheless, the soul, although entering in and remaining passively, absorbing purity and love, does not remain in it for the rest of its earthly life. It is aware of such depth as never before experienced, but nothing is 'seen' clearly, this cannot be. It may remain for great lengths of time but service to mankind is not at an end, but must be continued until life's end, when no longer physically capable, then prayer for mankind is utterly continuous until one's capabilities are finished, hopefully, until the moment of passing from this life, may love be within us, intercession and offering to God…I see this as a most blessed state, and as near as one may get in this earthly life to fulfilment…

Comment:

Ivy is now much more settled in the experience of "visionary" happenings and is able to express what is taking place more coherently without losing the sense that what is happening is ultimately beyond words. She is still not entirely able to grasp sometimes how a particular word could confuse the reader, for example, the word 'absorption', which she uses throughout her life, can be seen to have connotations of that loss of human identity which is prevalent in Hindu and Buddhist mysticism, but right at the start, she does explain clearly that for her the word means recognition that "the Father's house is contained in the Son, the way to the Father is through the Son" (7 May). This is a profound re-expression of the Christian belief that we are able to approach the Father through Jesus Christ Our Lord, revealing a depth of understanding of the meaning of the crucifixion, which goes beyond its significance as the place of atonement for sin.

All mystics develop their own technical language, some of which they hold in common with others, some of which are personal to them. One such personal word, which Ivy develops, is that of "the centre" at first with a slightly hazy meaning, signifying both something of the person and something of the grace of God. However, it rapidly develops into a clearer meaning, namely as the place in the human being where the human ability to reach out to God is met by the grace of God revealing himself to us. For most mystics, the word used for this is "soul" but for Ivy, the phrase "the centre" anchors the experience at the very heart of the human experience and avoids the dangers of the body/soul dichotomy which can undermine the truth that mystical experience at its best happens at the centre of our lives in the context of God's world. It also gives that experience an element of human co-operation with God's grace, so that, for example, she can say "the centre withdraws" from a time of visionary experience. What is expressed in "the centre" are the same as that expressed in the word "soul" i.e. the intellectual, emotional, intuitive components of human relationships, focused on the relationship with God and therefore recast into a form and attitude which can relate beyond words to the infinite, uncreated, eternal mystery of God. She relates the centre and the soul in a passage on 8 November 1978, when she writes, "The soul in one respect is a frail 'centre'…carried in the early stages hither and thither…it is up and down – the trough…the crest…like a butterfly settling here – settling there – a sip of nectar, then away alighting perhaps on something that does not contain nectar at all – it listens to all and sundry…practising this, then that…certain at different points it has found something that satisfies it…only after a while to discover that it is still 'hungry'…still 'thirsty'…it may practise religion all its life…and it may do many things that are good…Yet its 'centre' never fully opens and recognises that which it seeks…Because it fails to love fully…it loves all the good it performs and fails to 'see' who it is performing it for…consider the soul initially as a round opaque ball, when or if it overcomes all initial setbacks…and it will be beset by many, many things…'the centre' is finally pierced and it finds itself in the light of the 'house'." This quotation goes on to describe the development of 'the centre' of the soul into maturity through this new relationship with God. In fact, Ivy sees 'the centre' as the ability within the soul to move from the practice of formal and external religion into a living relationship with God, something which not everyone who believes finds.

Also, like all other mystics, Ivy is quite clear that although she uses the language of the senses – seeing, hearing, touching, smelling, tasting, imagining – yet in fact she sees nothing, hears nothing, etc. Using this language is no more than an analogy. Similarly, she uses the language of the emotions – joy, hope, fear, grief – to describe her experiences but again she is clear that although very aware of powerful 'emotions' in the vision, she is at the time unemotional.

Nevertheless, afterwards, the visionary experience may leave her exhausted because of the immensity of the vision and its revealed meaning.

Thirdly, Ivy, following the advice of St John of the Cross, does not trust her experience without having it validated by 'external authority' and she takes the 'visions' to her new spiritual director, The Revd Dr Martin Israel, for his consideration and assessment. The fact that he validates what she is experiencing means that she can proceed with assurance. What Ivy had not anticipated was that in seeking him out as her spiritual director, her influence on him was to grow to the point where he depended on her as significantly as she depended upon him. This we have seen in chapter 2.

We now move on to a selection of Ivy's 'visionary' experiences over the years leading to her move to Holbeach.

Chapter 4
Ivy's Inner Awareness

13 March 1989

There is for me at this time, ordinary everyday living, there are no highs, no lows, and equanimity in all things. There is continuing prayer and recollection, there are thoughts and remembrances of the past, plus a faint questioning of the future, there is no vision, it has been removed, there is no definite remembering of anything that was received, I am aware that it was so, but that is all. There are periods of physical weakness that I cannot account for, it is not all the time, however, but from time to time. Time itself speeds by, I am aware of my age, but do not dwell upon how much time is left. Today is bright, spring-like, a high wind, spring flowers are in bloom in the garden, new life as always overtakes the old. On further reflection, I am made aware of the necessity of prayer and intercession as an ongoing process of spiritual exercise. I realised this, more so because vision has been withdrawn, whether indefinitely or permanently I do not know, but when vision is experienced over a long period of time, it is very easy to depend upon it, and perhaps feel that without it, ordinary day-to-day prayer is not so valuable, so it is very important to accept the withdrawal, as it is to accept its presence when it is given, to be in a spiritual state of 'equanimity in all things', it is the fruit of inner peace, where inwardly there is a concern for God, and the things of God and for people and their needs, where love is the partner of truth and their discernment is given through the Spirit of wisdom. Without constant and unremitting prayer, this is not possible, it is not, however, a cocoon that protects against the world, the flesh and the devil, we live in the world and are called to combat all that may assail us. We are aided through faith, we live in hope, and prayer is that within, rising constantly within in supplication, 'Abba'.

(Ivy's mention of how much time she has left becomes far more pressing in the last years of her life as she longs to depart and be with God, but continues to remain alive despite her increasing ill health. See the last chapter)

24 October 1989

I returned home last Friday after two weeks, there has been much to-ing and fro-ing this summer, I have written of my visit to Lincolnshire in the other diary, as it concerns a probable move, and this is an important area of my life (if it should happen). I am, as always glad to be home, I can see that if one lived permanently with one's children, how easy it would be to lose not only independence but identity, one would be 'Mum' and 'Nana', not a person in one's own right. Many might say this could not happen, but I think otherwise.

12 February 1990

The acute awareness of inner loneliness has returned. This is not to be confused by the loneliness that plays such a painful part in many lives, the inability to mix with others, one's natural temperament that makes friendship difficult, the natural follow on of bereavement, divorce, so many reasons, coupled with this is usually depression, ills of mind and body. The inner loneliness I am referring to is of the soul, there appear to be degrees of it as the road is travelled, and the farther along the road, the more sensitive one becomes of its presence. I find it difficult to describe because in one sense it seems contradictory, one is aware of well-being, of alertness, of a clear mind etc, the fruits of a continuing inner and undisturbed peace, yet coupled with this is the knowledge that deep within one's own self is this seeking – a constant seeking that is never fully satisfied, it reminds me of a container of some sort that is never quite filled, human love never quite fills it, knowledge of beauty in whatsoever form it takes never quite fills it, always there is this emptiness that is ever-present deep within, strangely enough, it is not an unhappy state, if it were, then mind or body (or both) would be affected. One acknowledges its presence, accepts it as perhaps a necessary part of the road, then continues one's journey, it is not something to be dwelt on or queried.

12 June 1990

There has been a period over these last few days that could be called dereliction of spirit, the loneliness of spirit, yes, but dereliction is perhaps on a deeper level even to that, I am sure the root cause of this was the rejection received (*unspecified and not clear in earlier pages*) and this calls from the depths of one's being to look or try to look very clearly and with truth at oneself. I emphasise again that one must not reject in return, and this is very difficult to do, even knowing that it is the right course to take, but do it one must if one is to proceed in love. I thought deeply about rejection, not only mine but concerning all people. To be rejected on moral grounds, political grounds, because of poverty, of disease etc, I think is on a different level than on a personal one-to-one basis, where friendship has been deep over a number of years, and where it could be said that either side was allowed complete freedom of speech in such a friendship. I am only writing about myself here and not for the other person concerned, offers of help that have not been specifically asked, or asked for indirectly, must not be too surprised at being refused, although in this case there has been no refusal, there has been no acknowledgement at all and this has what has gone so deeply. But when I look within my own depths, I see pride rearing its head. This is what has so wounded me, once I have been brought face to face with this, all other things disappeared, now all is well. This does not, however, excuse the discourtesy of the other person concerned, and at some time in the future, it will be brought to their attention. I am very grateful to have been shown this.

1 August 1990

I do understand my spiritual road as a lonely one. Human need does raise its head from time to time and this is to be expected, yet it is the spiritual side that is far stronger, and indeed is getting stronger the older I become. Perhaps this particular time, I am faced with the final 'letting go', and as always, I fight every inch of the way what I know is inevitable. What complex beings we humans are, the old man takes a long time dying, there is little holding me now, a few final strands to be severed, we are given so much leeway by God, finally, however, all must be relinquished before all is given.

11 August 1990

When I last saw M.I. he spoke of the writing and thought it may be approaching its zenith, whether what has been written recently is the zenith, I do not know, it could well be, I have given some thought as to what may happen if/when I move; I have to leave that and wait and see, I have no way of knowing; I am sure it will not disappear altogether, there will be a day-to-day happenings, new people, descriptive writing, for it will all be completely different and I am ready to meet this. As far as all that has been written goes, all has been a learning process. I am not the same person either mentally or emotionally as when the first tentative jottings were put down in late 1969, I was immature in many ways, especially with regard to people, and certainly regarding all clerics, and all within contemplative or other Orders. I assumed they knew everything and were never uncharitable or untruthful – naïve in the extreme – when certain persons 'fell from their pedestals'. It was a very painful process as far as I was concerned, it taught me, however, about humanity, and it taught me about forgiveness and the love of God for all that he has created. Love should be limitless, we, however, are not God and this is a hard lesson to learn, it is difficult to a degree, but not impossible, when at the final reckoning such love has not achieved what it saw as the will of God, this does not mean it has failed, but that God has used it so as to teach it its meaning, so whoever finally reads the spiritual journals/diaries must bear in mind that what was written was what was given, whether by God or from some other source, so masked as not to be recognised for what it was, the insight, the imagination, etc. The gradual absorption of the whole being was given to it over many years and ran so to speak side by side with family life and all other areas of an ordinary working-class life, the life I was born into and the life in which I shall die. I regret nothing and would have nothing changed. I have had many glimpses into 'life that would be above my station' but I have not been inspired by what I have seen, theirs too is a difficult road. I love dearly my two sons and their children, I love even deeper my late husband, yet there has always been the feeling of 'apart'. I am not able to explain this, it is how it has always been, this is how it has always been with other people, with friendships that are dear to me and close to my heart, and yet 'apart'. I was prompted to write this quite suddenly and without previous thought, and at this point, I leave it.

18 October 1990

The word 'loneliness' has been uppermost in my mind for some time, as I have written before, I have been aware of it within myself for many years, I believe it was a road given to certain people by God, and perhaps one's natural temperament helps, many people would be unable to cope with it, in which case the meaning would never be clear to them. If this type of loneliness is experienced, it is recognised, perhaps not initially, but finally, it is recognised as the road God has given you for his own reasons. In the recognition, one opens oneself to be used, and this is what he will do if it is accepted, one has a choice, and yet if one chooses not to accept, then one's potential, one's gift (for this is what it is) is not fulfilled in the way it was intended to be. This has nothing to do with being lonely, or with being alone, 'lonely and alone' is often part of a depressive state from which it is often difficult to escape, but this 'loneliness of spirit' is an integral part of the whole person, in a spiritual sense one walks with God always, under all circumstances, in all life's trials and temptations that beset the person, they very seldom go deep enough to affect this or are able to dispel it, one share in a small way Christ's Gethsemane, in the midst of people there is silence and solitude. It was there for me personally throughout my marriage, it was, as I have already written, a happy marriage, laughter and fun running parallel with the upsets and tribulations of daily life, but deeper than any of this ran the thread of loneliness and this has never changed. With this comes an ever-growing non-attachment, one is always within it and yet remains outside it, as I have already written…This must be watched, one's response can become clinical, and this is not practising the love of Christ, there must be a balance, one may feel remote inwardly, but it must never be allowed to spill out on others so that you are seen as difficult to approach. (This is not finished, early tomorrow to Jeffrey and Lois for a week or so)

29 October 1990

Early this morning, I re-read what is written (above) on 'the loneliness of spirit'…Speaking for myself, one always feels apart from others, even when in their company, in some inexplicable way, one is cut off, I am unable to say whether this is experienced in the same way by kindred spirits, but this is how it is with me. Now, as the end of earthly life approaches, days? Months? Years? I welcome it, I intend to live whatever lies before me to the full, neither looking back nor forward to any great extent, but – even as I write this – this moment. I add yet again that what I have written (before) makes no difference at all to the knowledge of love as being compassionate to all, to try to listen, to understand, to be with them where they are and not where we think they should be, to put oneself in their shoes. I read a meaningful line in a book recently regarding doubt, difficulties with faith and prayer etc. "Is my gloom, after all, a shade of his hand?"

25 March 1991

If in writing I have made the transition (to Holbeach) sound effortless, this is not so, there have been no practical major catastrophes, and inwardly it has been easier than I thought it would be, the inner loneliness however is ever-present, even when with family, amid laughter discussions etc., it is there and I am aware of it, yet it must be an integral part of my make-up, for whoever I am with for any given time, I want to be alone. Humanity, and all that it gives, does not satisfy the inner longing for 'aloneness', so it really sounds like a contradiction in terms. Spiritually, one must hold on to Our Lord at all costs. There have been moments of self-pity, a little 'accidie' perhaps, as far as I am concerned, it is in recognition, seeing them for what they are, that the will to overcome must be exercised. I think I expect more from others than they are able to give; in my experience, no one is 'there for you' all the time, and if that is turned round, are we there for them all the time? I think not, there is only one person who does this, or is able to do this, and that is God. The words return to me, said to me many years ago (1968–69) by Fr Dominic Whitnall C.R. "Ivy, Ivy, clinging to the cross." I did not understand it then, spiritually I was very young, now, I understand and therein lies my strength. Deo gratias.

25 August 1991

There have been many days of interior emptiness, a time where prayer seems to be a mechanical process, at times like these, the first two words of the Lord's Prayer are sufficient, prayer should never be allowed to become a chore. This afternoon emptiness disappeared as though it had never been.

8 May 1992

Early morning…

'Loneliness, what is thy name?
Thy name is heartache.'

Chapter 5
Some Mature Visions from Ivy's Time in Walthamstow

The Blessed Virgin Mary
1978

2 February

Briefly within came thoughts of B.V.M…the motherhood of Mary, I held this as her going back over the road to find her young son!

3 February

After the 12.30pm mass yesterday, I lit a votive candle. I feel drawn towards her in a way, I have not been drawn before. For years, I have never felt anything regarding her, shrines have not touched me, perhaps the beginning came about six years ago when I was given a rosary, I learnt how to use it, and used it daily for about three years, yet at the same time it never brought me any closer to her as a mother or as the Mother of Our Lord, except for one thing, and that was the Pietà. I first became aware of this when going round the Cathedral in Amalfi in 1972. There is an enormous stone statue of this, I gazed and gazed upon it, almost unable to tear myself away, sometime after that I was given – by somebody, I did not know too well – a card for Easter of the Pietà…There are two things I always think of regarding the B.V.M., one – going to find her son and the realisation that must have come from this, that all children must grow up and leave the mother that bore them, ideally never leaving them within the heart, they are not one's possession and must be freed – and the second regarding the Pietà, the absolute agony she must have suffered as a mother, watching her son die upon the cross…I can think of nothing now more conducive to human suffering than a mother having to watch the death, sometimes the slow death, of a loved child…That Jesus handed over his mother to St John shows the depth of love he had for his mother and his awareness in his last agony that his mother was there, and this in it, that love must be free and must give freedom to the beloved, one of the most difficult things facing a mother is to really free her child. If this is done, then in reality the child does not leave, neither does she leave the child, they are bound in the heart…Motherhood in its truest form must be the purest love, the child is part of the mother as it can never be part of the father, the carrying of the child within, the birth and the immediate nourishment afterwards of the child, drawing still from the mother, may bind us as no other earthly relationship can. I must say at this point, I am only too aware of the lack of many mothers of motherhood in the truest sense, and of the suffering caused to many children in physical and emotional ways here, of possession that never frees the child, the result can be so stultifying as to kill love completely, and this happens over and over again with disastrous results.

If realisation can be given, or the child led in whatsoever way to the love of the heavenly Father, and relate through this to the motherhood of the Son and/or the motherhood of Mary, then they may be freed from the tie of the natural mother and the ensuing guilt and cleave to the real motherhood that gives always, but possesses not. In trying to look at myself, I realise that I have gradually come to rely on my intercessions to B.V.M., praying daily to her to intercede for me for love and wisdom regarding my own children, and with all others with whom I have become involved added to this has been prayer, asking her to intercede for others. This has been slow, but it has happened, yet she has never been as vivid to me as she is now becoming. I have tried to push it from me, but it returns until at this point, I find myself looking at her within myself for the first time with recognition…I see a person who accepted without question God's will, a simple person, and still – although in many circles acclaimed as the 'Queen of Heaven' etc, remaining a mother and not just a mother but The Mother – the chosen by the Father to bear the Son. After rearing him, to let him go to do the work he was sent to do, and if we are to try, and that is the operative word, to pattern ourselves as mothers on this, it is to let our children go, to remain in the background, being ready if needed to be used, not to intrude. And so, the Holy Mother was, accepting, loving, in her simplicity and gentleness, unassuming, she waits, at his death, she was there…I am sure there was a deep bond between Our Lord and his mother that needed no words, the child is forever in the mother's heart. The mother to the child is what? Mother!

21 February

After saying the Hail Marys this morning, the Holy Mother again came before me, and I found myself saying within myself, "Teach me to accept with humility God's will." On our acceptance so much hinges, because when we say to ourselves, or assure ourselves to ourselves "I accept" whatever the relationship is, the situation is, etc, it does not always bring spiritual and emotional and mental relief because we fail to accept ourselves in it, it is very difficult indeed to view oneself in truth in a difficult relationship, for example, we see very clearly the other person, the kind of person they are, what they have done and perhaps are still doing to us, the heartache and suffering we have endured, and at the bottom of this lack of acceptance of self, lies guilt, they are guilty, but one's own guilt lies in our inability to forgive us ourselves because we fail to love them. A priest said to me many years ago, "you are wearing a hair shirt." I wore this hair shirt for many years and unconsciously, I think it became my Bona fide because to myself in my reactions to this relationship, again and again, I flayed myself with it, but what I failed to do was to take it off. I failed to see myself clearly in this relationship. I failed to understand the real love of God, I was afraid, fear is very deep-rooted, so deep-rooted in fact, that if taxed with it we would probably deny it. Basic fear breeds guilt, and it is well-nigh impossible to accept the person in question – much less ourselves in the relationship, without understanding God's love, and the only way to do this is through his crucified Son. God's will in giving us these relationships leads us ultimately to the realisation of ourselves, they may practically annihilate us in the process, but keeping our inward eye ever open on the ultimate end – which is Christ – we do overcome. Acceptance, true acceptance, does bring peace, it is seeing God in the situation, not oneself…On a more practical side, it often does a lot of good to sit down quietly and try to look at the other person, ask oneself why they are as they are, is it possible for them to change? Yes, it is possible for them to change or be changed, but first of all their own eyes must be open to themselves and in many unchristian minds it is not going to happen and probably you/me or whoever is not going to be able to change them anyway, so accept that fact. In their own guilt, all they want to do is to transfer it to someone else in an effort to free themselves. They often do manage to transfer it, much to the suffering of the receiver, but they are never free, their only freedom lies in the crucified one, and mostly their hearts and minds are shut to him. This must be recognised, it is useless banging one's head against a brick wall, be kind, be dutiful, remembering them daily in prayer before God, because in him lies the answer, not only for them but for ourselves in the realisation of real love, and the icicle that for many years has been our heart (in relation to who oppresses us) slowly melts into Christ's redeeming love...The Holy Mother within, accepting without question the will of God...

29 May 1979

My prayer at the altar rail is for an increase in love and prayer. At the receiving, the centre is pierced...the soul appears as a 'ground', a mixture of weeds, nettles, with here and there a bloom struggling to survive, the awareness of the centre...the core...comes from the receiving of Our Lord, it pierces the centre releasing the dormant love...the dormant longing for God which we hitherto have not understood or had a name for...at each receiving...if we truly desire to know God. The core which houses the 'well' living in us all, will rise to the surface and very slowly begin to flood the 'ground'...the blooms there will be strengthened the more...the weeds and nettles will succumb...the roots will slowly disintegrate and fade, to be finally absorbed into the 'ground'. They do not do so with ease of grace...they are extremely loathe to go, and will fight for survival in a hundred ways...the antidote is in the receiving...the constant piercing...and the desire and will to know God, there is no other way...the 'ground' takes on new meaning and becomes warm, an open channel that draws to it...it becomes changeless, able to give constantly, drawing its own sustenance from the 'well'. As the 'ground' becomes totally submerged, it is totally obedient to the Father...there is of course during this learning and striving, an overlapping from earthly life to the life beyond...total perfection only comes from the fire to the flame and its subsequent journey...but the 'ground' in this life may be changed out of all recognition through its desire and longing for God, through his Son Jesus Christ...in depth, a return of the souls borne along...towards the Father...(This is what was received in prayer with M.I.) It goes no farther yet, just awareness of vast silence...

30 May

The receiving...the centre pierced...the 'water' overflows onto the 'ground', which is irrigated and nourished...

31 May

Mass...a repetition of the above...silence...rapt, a line appears in my mind "Underneath are the everlasting arms"...warmth.

2 June

Mass...the centre pierced...the nourishing of the 'ground'...warmth...seven veils...silence...

3 June

Mass...the receiving...the centre pierced covers the 'ground'...warmth...seven veils? A veiling? The congregation of souls...to be accompanied through each veil...each veil a showing in light...the 'guardian' of the veils...who accompanies the souls through each veil...at this point a clear picture of the Holy Mother...she carries in her arms the infant Christ...it faded leaving me in the complete silence of the mind.

4 June

The escort of the congregation of souls within the first veil by the Holy Mother 'Guardian'. This is the veil of love...here the souls are taught and are shown the meaning of Divine Love...I am not shown this and cannot know it until I reach this myself...I am only aware at this point that this is what is shown to them...the Holy Mother carries in her arms the infant Christ...he is the teacher...here in this veil the souls receive raiment...they are clothed...and their clothing is love...they may dwell here for a long time...my inward eye is upon the Teacher...and in the infant Christ lives the Father...'underneath are the everlasting arms'...In the awareness of love, the congregation of souls worship...silence...the hosts of the heavenly beings that have accompanied the souls from the emerging from fire to flame...that have emanated joy and thanksgiving, are not present here...all is 'seen'...'understood'...'taught' and 'learnt' in silence…but it is not the silence that is known on this earth…it is the Divine Silence that 'speaks' of the meaning of Divinity…my mind is in silence and I rest…

6 June

Prayer…The souls now clothed pierce the second veil, the veil of perception…they are fully protected by their clothing, it is their armour. The Guardian bearing the Christ child precedes them…silence…The Teacher fully enhances their understanding…and 'teaches' their hitherto sightless eyes. He shows the earth, not as they lived upon it, this has already been dealt with, but the whole earth…timelessness…the light and the dark…The final fulfilment of the Father's will…the perfection of love…They are made aware of the evil pervading the earth, of man's failure to love…looking upon the Christ child (the Teacher) they 'see' man's redemption, they also 'see' the Father within him and at the moment of recognition their armour is pierced by his suffering as he beholds the earth and all he made therein…'Underneath are the everlasting arms'…in which the earth is held…without which the earth would not exist…the souls worship…silence…silence.

7 June

At the receiving, the centre pierced overflows and waters the 'ground'…it is absorbed leaving the 'ground' empty of all things, barren…a wasteland – the soul resents nothing of this, it is happy in its state of nothingness…parallel to this the congregation of souls are held within the second veil. The Holy Mother holds the Christ child and they worship him…for the duration of the Mass, this was within me.

25 June

At the receiving the ground is flooded and the life-giving water is absorbed into the barrenness of the soul…this barrenness is not in the accepted sense, although it is barren…empty…yet it is rich in the quality of the soil, it is detached from all things of this world and continued completely in the centre of light (The Trinity). While the souls in the second veil intercede for those on earth, the 'Guardian', in whose hands the child is held, subtly changes in as much as the child is absorbed into her, to be replaced by the third member of the Holy

Trinity…the Dove…it is the same 'Teacher'? Later, it returned at this point…the earth and all there faded from the souls' sight…all darkened and faded…the only light to them was in their beholding of the 'Guardian' in whose hands rested the Dove…silence, there is nothing except awareness of worship…the 'guardian' rests…the Dove rests in the Holy Mother…the veil lightens as it awaits the parting of the next veil.

26 June

The lifting of the 3rd veil. The 'guardian' enters, bearing in her hands the Dove…this veil is the veil of truth…the souls here are shown by the Holy Spirit the complete life of Our Lord Jesus Christ while upon earth…it is revealed to their understanding, from within the womb of the Holy Mother to the crucifixion…all that we are ignorant of in this world…or assume has or has not taken place, is shown to them in truth…all is fully opened to them and absorbed by them…from the beginning of Our Lord's passion…to his actual last breath, is not shown to them as they understood it in this world…or as those in this world now understand it, but it is as a reversal…they are shown it in Divine Light and understand it from within Our Lord…there is no 'body', but the light that dwelt and dwells within the body, the body dies (has died) leaving exposed the true light that is Christ…they are shown again the earth in darkness and in light…temporal darkness to be superseded by Divine Light…the souls absorb the teaching of the Holy Spirit…rest…thanksgiving and prayer…The light is revealed to the souls, and containing truth, is not light as we know it…it is transparency in which is contained the heart of the Trinity.

27 June

Prayer…Spiritual Communion…The souls are led by the Holy Spirit into the sepulchre in which the Lord's body was laid…they perceive by Divine revelation the disintegration of the outward body (darkness) leaving exposed the sacred heart contained in transparent light…They travel with it…led by the Spirit, to the distinct place of the Father's will…there the Lord reveals himself as the Son of God…at this point, my inward eye is aware of the Holy Mother…the Guardian of the veils…complete silence…wonder!

161

1 July

Mass...during this time, one line intruded and continued to do so..."The ground of thy bestowing!" The continuation of the souls in the third veil...as they are made aware of the revelation of himself (Jesus Christ) as the Son of God...there comes also at this point knowledge of a 'dark place'...it is in the cloud at this time and the souls are not aware of it...the Holy Spirit does not enter...I meditated a little on this...it is perhaps the abode of the unredeemed...but I do not see it as being so forever...there is no sound or crying...Rather like a place of waiting...it is perhaps the separation...the hardest to endure...The souls seek rest...The 'Guardian', bearing in her hands the Dove...the line returns 'the ground of thy bestowing'. It clears, revealing the Holy Mother in truth...She is the 'ground' that retained the seed and from whom came forth the flower of perfection...'the ground of thy bestowing'...rest.

2 July

Prayer...the souls continue to be shown truth as revealed to them by the Holy Spirit...there is no awareness of time, but rather of timelessness...there is awareness though of the clothing of the souls...as the Divine Truth is made known to them, so does this clothing deepen in the texture of light...the souls are conducted at this point to the seventh and last veil...the veil of fulfilment, but they do not pierce it...rather do they 'see' into it...it is here that the sacred heart, contained in light, enters to be absorbed into the Father...the receiving by the Son of the benediction of the Father...a brief uniting before his return to the world...the resurrection...in fulfilment of the will of God...before the final uniting of the Son to the Father, the souls receive the knowledge, the piercing of their understanding, they return to the third veil...the 'Guardian' waits for their return...then in gentleness as the guardian surveys the souls...rest, the Dove within her hands. Later, in little meditation, I understand more fully how love must be...it is in the Divine...contained in all...first love...clothed in love...love and perception...love and truth...love.

3 July

Mass...at the receiving, the 'ground' is flooded, but it is quickly absorbed...The souls are led by the Holy Spirit...they are shown the earth and the resurrected body of Christ upon it...they are aware of the inner light that is life...he has returned to conclude his mission according to the will of the Father...at the appointed time he ascends to the Father, travelling from time to timelessness...to the seventh veil of fulfilment, which he enters and is one with God...the glorious light within this veil pierces outwards, permeating the heavens...it travels swiftly back through all veils until it reaches he 'dark place'...this it pierces, releasing the imprisoned, who are then escorted back to the beginning of the decent of the narrow beam and must go through all subsequent places of learning and repentance...these were perhaps what were known as the damned...those who turned from God...those under the power of the evil one...but I 'see' that even these – in God's time, and according to his will, cannot bide forever in darkness, no darkness presided over by the evil one can survive once pierced by the love that is Christ...nothing is immediate, and by that I mean in any foreseeable future...it cannot be in human imagination...it is as vast clouds rolling and rolling beyond sight and literally into eternity...The Dove returns to rest in the hands of the 'Guardian'...the souls also rest and ponder...peace...

6 July

The Lord's Prayer...'Thy kingdom comes'...the Hail Mary's the Holy Mother the Guardian of the veils...an awareness of gentleness...also enigmatic mystery an awareness of human reasoning...acceptance of what is given...Not for questioning 'how' from thence to the third veil...the 'Guardian' is enclosed here in an aura of light...she precedes the souls and pierces the fourth veil which is the veil of sorrow...she is alone inasmuch that she is 'seen' to be alone, yet there is knowledge of the 'unseen' presence...not Christ...Not the Dove...But the Godhead...the souls are silent in their adoration...from the aura surrounding the Holy mother is transmitted the 'word' to the souls...silence...depth...they are led to the dark place wherein resides evil...they are not at this point allowed to 'see' the imprisoned...only evil; and the resulting horrors...these are magnified many times to their knowledge of evil on earth...they are shown that here is the root...gnarled, twisted and deformed...spiritually deformed, as the full realisation enters their understanding they know sorrow...not only their own...but the sorrow of the Creator...it envelops them momentarily...and they weep...

9 July

The 'Guardian' surrounded by the aura leads the souls from the 'dark place' to another viewing of the world...there they 'see' the fruit of the evil contained in the 'dark place', its tentacles spread throughout the earth...in every place, no place is exempt...They are viewed as dark rivers...black rivers, their streams and tributaries everywhere...affecting all peoples of the earth, there being no exception of class, creed or colour...they are aware of the insidiousness of the evil one, cunning and devious in his invading of souls, and his possession of them...A man may fall through many factors...They are made aware of the pain and tears of the innocent who suffers through no fault of their own...the tears of the souls...the tears of the souls fall as gentle rain...the 'guardian' withdraws leaving them to ponder...

11 July

Prayer...The souls are led by the 'Guardian', who remains within the aura of Divine Light, once more to the 'dark place' wherein resides the root of evil...they are shown the enormity of its growth, the ugliness of it and the changeability of it as it works itself to represent good...the deadliness of it as it invades the souls in the world...the souls in this veil themselves are fully protected by their clothing...it is not themselves that can now be touched...but they weep afresh for mankind's...rest.

13 July

(In retreat at Pleshey conducted by M.I.)

At the receiving, the 'ground' was flooded...it breaks forth into bloom before again being made barren...The souls still within the fourth veil, the veil of sorrow...the 'guardian' surrounded by the aura beholds them...The souls behold the 'guardian'...in silence the aura transfers from the 'guardian' to the souls, they are surrounded by it and filled with it...their clothing is pierced as an arrow pierces...they are led to view the earth and behold upon it the crucified Christ...they are filled with the sorrow of the Father as he not only beholds...but is with the pain of the Son. The aura withdraws, leaving them in deepest sorrow...they are pierced and the wound at this point is not healed...they behold and they weep...rest...In the depth of their sorrow do they behold the heart of the Saviour...and they worship...

18 July

Mass this morning…at the receiving the 'ground' is flooded…this time the waters do not recede, but instead rose higher and higher…the centre (rather unprepared for this) was carried upon the waters to the 4th veil…there was expectancy within the centre! The souls were expectant before the 'Guardian', she waits and within her hands is the Dove…the aura is no longer around her, it resides within her…the aura is no longer around the souls, it resides within them…they have become one within the heart of Christ and it is here that they are held and pierced by the sorrow…they have been drawn into it and partaken from it…it lives within them and they live within the heart…In the sorrow of the Father have they partaken and of the Son, and they are changed, the centre beholds this, but cannot be part of it. When its time comes, it too must traverse the whole of the road to this point and beyond. The 'Guardian', holding in her hands the Dove, precedes the souls out of the 4th veil, the veil of sorrows and pierces the 5th veil, the veil of faith and hope…one cannot make one word of faith and hope, but they must remain as one, or perhaps rather in myself they are one, as love is in all the veils…they are one, all is one…once more the 'Guardian' leads the souls to view the earth…but it is in light…it is transfigured before them…and they are transfigured within it…the stream of living water proceeds from it…from the side, beneath the heart, does it proceed and it runs into the earth…it traverses the earth in all places and in all parts…as a silver stream (it) runs forth…there seemed great darkness (evil) had almost overtaken the earth…it rose high as mountains, its depth seemed unfathomable, it lay over the earth like a great pall, suffocating and putrid…the Dove left the hands of the 'Guardian' and it descended in the souls' sight into the seeming abyss…rest…intercession.

19 July

I woke early…made a cup of tea and took it back to bed – I was fully relaxed, I knew the next veil was to be wisdom, but my mind was completely empty. I said the Lord's Prayer and began the Hail Mary's, I did not get far. The centre travelled of its own accord to the 5th veil, the veil of faith and hope…the souls await the coming of the 'Guardian'…she is before them bearing within her hands the infant Christ…she precedes the souls into the 6th veil…the veil of wisdom…she turns to the souls and holds forth the infant Christ…they are filled…for before them is the Wisdom of God contained within his Son, Our

Lord Jesus Christ…worship…the 'Guardian' withdraws, the infant Christ (the Teacher) leads the souls to the beginning of time…'before Abraham was, I am'…the universe and all contained therein unfolds before them…the growth of it…mountains, rivers, seas, forest and desert…creatures of the earth and their place upon it…the ages are open to them…the kings, the scribes and prophets…humanity in its strength and weakness…its loves and hates…its rise and fall, its rise and fall…its rise and fall (lies) before them like a vast scroll being unrolled…the leaders of God's people…the chosen in every age are as lights upon the way…the darkness and evil growth from the beginning lies exposed to their understanding…there is nothing that has not been opened to them…the harshness of law without love, the sacrifice of the innocent, the sacrifice by so many of all but their own self…the hand of the Creator in every age and showing itself in the inexplicable as well as the obvious…so they are led into the knowledge of wisdom to be contained within the immaculate conception…they withdraw and are still…rest…Prayer, the souls wait…the 'Guardian' bears the infant Christ within her hands, she faces the souls and holding him forth presents him and they behold Wisdom. Every veil is filled with the sound of praise and thanksgiving, the veils are surrounded and filled with the heavenly beings, and light envelops them…rest…the souls wait upon the 'guardian'…Silence (within myself this appeared to continue for a long time)…The 'Guardian' presents herself before them…she is alone, she precedes them from the 6th veil, the veil of wisdom, but before entering the 7th veil, the veil of fulfilment, she turns to them and their eyes are fully opened as they behold the Mother of Christ…and in their beholding, she was shown within the 7th veil, the veil of fulfilment…the souls do not enter here, the time is not yet…they rest and await the glory that is to be…Thanks be to thee, Almighty God.

This is written in the moment of time as upon the earth, but it means timelessness…not of this earth…the souls do not enter each veil in this sense…but in the timelessness of eternity…I do not understand fully, one is not able to understand this…I have written this as received. This is late afternoon on Thursday, the retreat finishes after breakfast tomorrow.

29 August

Prayer…an inward picture of the Host and Chalice…this has happened twice in the last couple of days…today the Holy Mother is present. She turns and I

166

know I must follow her. I do not 'see' the moment she is no longer there…only that I realise that she has gone.

30 August

Mass…the Host and Chalice…appearance of the Holy Mother, she turned and I followed…there was no light but I felt peace…again she was no longer there. Within my mind were the faces of certain dead people as I remembered them on earth…they were all people that I remembered as giving me pain…many were faces I remembered in childhood…they all passed through my mind…I felt nothing except peace…after a while, other faces followed…faces of those I had loved…as I knelt there I realised what I was receiving…it was nothing to do with anything I have consciously asked, a prayer for…except for my mother…she was the only exception…and her face was there among the others…I felt literally engulfed in a wave of prayer…not my prayer, but their prayer…and this widened and deepened to a knowledge of those on earth and those who are not now on the earth…and the souls' constant prayer for us who are here and who are so in need…as I came through this the faces returned…The faces of those that had given me pain, and the peace that was now already within me was overpowering…words formed in my mind 'The reconciliation with the dead'…rest…thanksgiving.

2 September

Yesterday to Walsingham. I'm afraid I still have mixed feelings about it…so many people around…so many different parties…I really cannot seem to either 'see' or 'find' the Holy Mother in all this…at first, I felt restless and rather anti…during the Mass at 3 pm it settled a little…and also during Benediction…but on the whole, I was happy when the time came to leave. I will talk to DT about this when I see him next Friday.

6 September

Prayer is constant, but I seem to be waiting, the Holy Mother leads, I follow, she withdraws, my prayer remains "Father, show mercy"…I am very busy. Regarding people, in fact, life at present is too rushed, but it will pass…I would not like this for too long and physically it would soon prove too much.

11 September

Prayer has been a repetition of the Holy Mother, she turning and I follow…Sunday at Mass it clarified…at the receiving, immediate awareness of the Holy Mother…in clear light…never before, or very rarely have I been conscious of colour, but today…purity…white, she was robed in white…she turned and I followed…at a certain point I realised she had entered something? There was nothing to be 'seen', I knew though that she had not 'gone' in the sense felt before but that she had entered 'into'. I knew I must follow, yet I did not do so…but retreated back…words came I did not fully understand and which I can only describe as a "Bower"…something of beauty…the abode of the Holy Mother…intercession.

12 September

Prayer, the Lord's Prayer…the Hail Mary's began, but at reaching "The Lord is with you," there was an awareness of her. Spiritual Communion…she was present here, bearing in her hands the infant Christ. She turned and I followed…there was serenity…joy…light…she entered an abode! She was met here by a myriad of 'Guardians'…an innumerable escort of 'lights'. These are the souls of the Holy Innocents…the 'Guardians' of the Holy Mother's abode in the Heavenly bodies. She moved inwards…? Rest.

14 September

Prayer…intercession…Spiritual Communion…the Holy Mother bearing in her hands the infant Christ purity…she leads me to a place! I follow…she passes 'through' to be surrounded by the 'Guardians', the souls of the Holy Innocents. As I recognise this, I am aware of learning? That here is wisdom in depth…the whole opens out before me…escorted by the 'Guardians' that are as brilliant pinpoints of light, she proceeds inwards and turning, still holding the infant Jesus, she is seated as in a bower…I find this difficult to describe in words…It is a place of innocence…unsoiled, yet in this innocence…or perhaps within it, is the wisdom of creation…here are contained the souls of the infants…all that have lived within the womb are here…They are borne here at clinical death upon the narrow beam and are under the care of the Holy Mother…there are myriads upon myriads of pin point lights…but all have their appointed place…the lights that are the Holy Innocents are brighter by far and easily distinguishable from all others…they never leave the place, but wait upon the Holy Mother, escorting her to and from the entrance when she proceeds to all the other veils over which she is the 'Guardian' and all the chambers contained there. All that the souls are taught within the other veils are taught here…but there is a marked difference…the souls travelling through the veils have sinned in the world and have finally reached the veils through the ways already described but the infant souls, based on the age of the Holy Innocents at clinical death have not sinned. They are chosen by the Father to be the lights of Heaven and are already pure. Their teacher is the infant Christ held within his Mother's arms and through him is imparted all learning, but this is far higher in degree because they are without spot…on a conscious thought comes the line 'unless you be as a little child you cannot enter the Kingdom of Heaven' and 'if anyone has looked into the eyes of an infant…the deep pools of knowledge that are contained there.'…but this is my own thought only. The Holy Mother rises and surrounded by the 'Guardians' proceeds inwards…the infant souls surround her as she passes from light into a darker place…yet the darker place is light also…there just seems a faint transitional stage…to a place that is almost as the first chamber…but there is a subtle difference…the centre withdraws…rest.

15 September

Mass…the receiving…the centre follows the Holy Mother into the second chamber…the centre is very aware of 'motherhood'…the Mother as in relation to the infant souls…here reside the souls of children as opposed to infants…they too, on clinical death are carried along the narrow beam…but although there is no comparison in the sins they have committed to those of responsible age, nevertheless they are not totally pure and without blemish, therefore they must be shown this, here again, the infant Christ is the teacher…There came a clear picture at this point of the crucified Christ! The young souls are in sorrow…their understanding is pierced as they turn from the infant to the man and the man to the infant…their young lives are open before them and in tears of regret they are gathered for comfort to the Holy Mother…the light dimmed and there was an awareness that in this embrace they slept…I found this at first rather odd…but it was a night of sleep as opposed to resting…but sleep is healing…when they awake they are changed…the centre is extremely moved by this and withdraws…rest.

16 September

Prayer...immediate Spiritual Communion...the centre follows the Holy Mother in inner silence...they travel to the 2nd chamber. A great myriad of lights welcome her...surrounded by them on every hand, she turns...within her hands rests the Dove...led by the brighter lights of the Holy Innocents, she proceeds into the 3rd chamber! Never on any level has the centre experienced anything like this...it withdraws.

17 September

Prayer...the centre immediately aware of the presence of the Holy Mother...Spiritual Communion in which the Holy Mother is always present...she turns...the centre follows to the 3rd chamber...there seem to be two divisions, the divider is a pure stream of water, there is no beginning and no end that can be 'seen', it comes from? And flows to? There is an apparent bank or edge, there is complete and deep silence as the centre is shown this...The Holy Mother withdraws into shadow...nevertheless she is present, the Dove hovers...the centre withdraws also, but not from the chamber, it becomes aware of myriads of lights going towards the water...they are immersed in it...there seems to be wave upon wave of them, and yet there is never too many for the stream to hold...knowledge enters the centre...knowledge of complete healing for them all...there are the baptised and the unbaptised...those of physical and mental abnormality as they were upon earth...the blind, deaf and dumb, the ones with Down's Syndrome, ones with cerebral palsy'...all those that suffered any loss...the orphan, the unwanted...They merged with all the other souls that had not suffered in these ways...as the centre watched, there was a subtle change within the water...like a ribbon running through it and the flame...the Dove hovered and the myriads of lights crossed through the division to the far side...the chamber was filled with light infusing every part...there was no apparent height, depth or width...no beginning, no end...the whole was one light of the merging of the souls. There came a sweet sound of a childish song, of joy...the centre at this point had to withdraw...rest.

19 September

Prayer...intercession...thanksgiving...Spiritual Communion...The centre followed the Holy Mother to the 3rd chamber...bearing the Dove within her hands she proceeds to the 4th chamber…she is escorted by the lights of the Holy Innocents and enters…the chamber is alive with the lights that are the souls of children…They wait for her coming. There is a gentleness about her being…love…She appears to sit as in a bower, the light dims around her – silence. Although not 'seen', her presence is known to be there…the light fades, darkens and from the furthest recesses of the chamber comes a figure…the waiting lights of the young children surround him…there is no limitation of space or light…the souls seem endless, and yet the chambers absorb all. The figure enters fully into the light and is known to be St Joseph. He turns to embrace the children before leading them into knowledge…they are still…receptive, and their understanding is pierced…He leads them to the moment of Christ's birth and from there through every issue of his childhood until the time he sits among the elders of the temple…nothing is kept from the souls…all things that have been hidden or unexplained is made known to them…this teaching in all its aspects is very important…as in Our Lord's childhood, they are shown reflections of their own. The moment of time within the temple is the bridge from childhood to adulthood…silence…the lights are still…the figure of St Joseph recedes and is absorbed back 'into'…The Holy Mother is within their midst, within her hands is the Dove…rest.

22 September

Prayer. Spiritual Communion. The centre follows the Holy Mother bearing in her hands the Dove, to the 4th chamber, the myriads of lights are gathered within…she proceeds to the opening of the 5th chamber but turns before entering…there is a great light illuminating all…the Dove leaves the hands of the Holy Mother and touches each light (soul) present…it imparts the twin gifts upon each of love and wisdom…they are impregnated with them…there comes a tremendous release of perception…joy…thanksgiving…there are the souls of children…and children they remain…here is nothing shown me regarding knowledge given them of the remainder of Christ's life on earth…only up to his time among the elders of the temple…but the wisdom conferred upon them by the Holy Spirit is of a depth not in proportion to a child's understanding…but far beyond this…I can only deduce from this that true wisdom does not come…or is given, with age alone, but is within the frailty of innocence…rest…Prayer, The Holy Mother, bearing in her hands the Dove, proceeds to the 5th chamber, she is surrounded by the myriads of lights…they are led to view the earth…and upon the earth the children...these are their concern, children in every circumstance enter their perception and understanding...children in abject poverty and distress...the abused...Physically and mentally crippled...The wayward...every facet of childish suffering is shown them...the evil present in its most malignant form upon the earth is not shown them...but the result of it present in the children are. They are shown the entire earth...all children of every caste, colour and creed...which has no meaning here...Children are looking upon children...they return to the Holy Mother...where within her embrace they weep...the centre withdraws.

24 September

Prayer...The prayer of the children for the children! The Holy Mother proceeds to the 6th chamber...she is accompanied by the myriads of lights...the silence within is total...the lights seem withdrawn? They are in awe...this did not last long, the centre withdrew...prayer...intercession.

27 September

Prayer...Spiritual Communion...the centre follows the Holy Mother to the 6th chamber...she turns, within her hands rests the Dove. The myriads of lights are around her...they are in awe...they wait upon? Silence. very gradually there is an intrusion of light...it fills the chamber...the lights that are the souls pale before it...they are as candle flames before the sun's rays...they are totally infused within the light and within this comes recognition...'Father'...the centre is aware of the whole of the light receding...yet also, that although the myriads of lights are now contained within the 'whole' light, they are being led and they follow in Joy...rest.

30 September

Mass...Communion...the centre follows the Holy Mother to the 6th chamber...the myriads of lights now contained within the 'whole' light is receding from the 6th chamber...they are joined again by St Joseph who with the Holy Mother precedes the 'whole' light, leaving this chamber they enter 'into' rest...later, prayer...The centre observes as the 6th chamber recedes and St Joseph and the Holy Mother enter a place! It is filled with the souls who wait in the 6th chamber...the veil of wisdom...the myriads of lights now contained within the 'whole' light, leave it (the 'whole' light)…the light withdraws beyond the 7th veil, the veil of fulfilment…and the lights that are the souls of children merge within the waiting souls…the Holy Mother and St Joseph are surrounded by the 'lights of heaven'…the souls of the Holy Innocents…there is intense joy and love in the mingling of all the souls…the joy of spiritual recognition…nothing of their earthly lament is known here…all are changed, yet there is a deep awareness of re-uniting, there is peace and there is love…all are purified, so in this recognition and in this re-uniting no stain remains, no remembrance of earthly trials remain…this is the final gift by the Father before the last and most glorious veil opens to receive them. St Joseph and the Holy Mother with the infant 'lights of Heaven' withdraw from there…rest…intercession.

1 October

Prayer…Spiritual Communion…the presence of the Holy Mother, the centre follows her to a place of light…the Holy Mother passes beyond the light…the centre stays within it! Silence…it remains within it.

3 October

Prayer…intercession…Spiritual Communion…there Holy Mother present here…the centre follows her to a place of light…it follows her through this for what seemed to be a long time, it passed through waves of light and darkness…light and darkness…until the Holy Mother was no longer present, the centre returned to the place of light where it remained…

5 October

Prayer…Spiritual Communion…the centre follows the Holy Mother, repetitive of the above…the waves of light and darkness were strong…there seemed a going back…the centre 'comes upon' the Holy Mother kneeling before her crucified son…in no way was the centre a part of this…it was shown it, this again was repeated…awareness of complete affinity…Prayer…the centre followed the Holy Mother to a place! There came a picture within of a journey to the Father…the soul at death was not carried along the narrow beam, as were the pure souls of the Holy Innocents. The narrow beam invaded the soul and travelled with it to beyond the seventh veil...the veil of fulfilment, where, ever obedient to the Father, it serves.

9 October

Last weekend to Walsingham with DT and parish, apart from the beginning when I felt very up tight, it was a lovely weekend. I still don't particularly want to go, certainly not for a long time...nevertheless, much good came from it, firstly the priestly role, so much love and care for his people, it emanated from him and his Priesthood was there for all to see and receive from. I realised literally quite suddenly, how important his Priesthood is, and how it must be protected at all costs, this is his true vocation, it came over loud and clear. Secondly, I met one of the parishioners who has a son of 19 years, with cerebral palsy. He came with us, he is totally unable to do anything at all for himself; we talked at great length, a sharing spiritually as well...

16 February – 5 March 1980, the Cross and the Water

Prayer...the crucifix to the forefront of my mind...This was replaced by a great expanse of water which, as it gradually receded, I followed, it became smaller and smaller until it became one single drop. The picture within of Christ crucified reappeared, the face itself becoming the focal point, the one drop of water upon it...a single tear! Mass, the fall of the tear...it is carried by the Dove! Late at night, spiritual communion, the Dove holds the tear of Christ...it shines like a precious jewel...the Dove begins a journey!

Mass, the Dove bearing the tear of Christ travels to the seventh veil, the veil of fulfilment...there is nothing 'seen' by the centre, rather a knowledge of the entrance of the Dove into the seventh veil where the tear of his beloved son is taken by the Father into his being...the tear is split, it separates into two, the Dove receives back one part, and leaving the seventh veil travels towards the place of the Holy Mother...the bower of the Holy Innocents...rest.

Mass, prayer...depth...the centre pierced travelled unhesitatingly to the Dove who bears the tear of Christ...the centre knew within itself the next step in the Dove's journey, but this did not happen...the Dove did not travel...it dropped the tear enclosing the centre within it...there was no 'feeling' as such, there was an immediate sense of total commitment, calm as not experienced before...a sense of it being so...this remained and is still within...Thanksgiving...joy.

The centre has been very quiet within itself, undisturbed…Prayer, Spiritual communion…the Dove enters the bower of the Holy Mother bearing the tear of Christ…she receives the tear which again parts into two…it is absorbed within her, the Dove leaves, bearing the residue…rest. Prayer, the centre is aware of the Dove bearing the tear, it travels through the earth alighting at given points, desert…mountains…river, they are remote points, but this is of no consequence, the tear splits again and again as the Dove releases the tear into the world, the tear, as 'seen' by the centre, is not the prerogative of Christians, although it will be unrecognised for what it is, it nevertheless floods the earth, touching all manner of people and instigating love and compassion within them, it will never 'dry up' in the sense that water may for many reasons 'dry up', but remains forever on the earth until the earth shall cease to be…the darker the earth may become because of the force of evil…the greater the power of the tear will be…it will not be overcome…the centre withdraws…later, prayer…intercessions…

(This vision clearly depends on former ones and did develop further, but is also freestanding in its completeness and its interpretation of the work of the Cross, as turning the sea of sin in the world into the teardrop of love and compassion that redeems the world.)

The River of Love

20 April 1983

(In retreat at St Mary's Abbey, West Mailing) My inner thought here is centred on the movement of love…the continuous flow…its strength and power when combined with truth…it's a never-failing endeavour to give of itself to all. Have spent some time on and off looking from my window. Although the weather is horrible, yet the beauty of it all overrides that.

One can never begin to imagine the depth of the unfolding of love as we are opened more and more to receive it, and the unfolding as we are enabled more and more to give. My prayer in chapel this evening was centred entirely on love…and the words, "Here am I, Lord, send me" are for me to give to others all that I have received. I 'saw' an inner picture of a river…it flows evenly, the water is pure and unsullied and totally clear, it is the water of love. Within the water and rising far above it were two enormous rocks. They were covered with footholds and finger holds where man has clung for sustenance from the beginning of time…and is clinging still. They are the rocks of faith and hope, rooted forever in love. I see the time spent here as a renewal 'to love unconditionally'…There is one rider, however, to be added. Love must know truth…it must have discernment, and it must always allow people or situations to go when wisdom shows this as necessary.

24 April

During prayer, the river of love with the twin rocks of faith and hope. The rocks crumbled into pieces and were absorbed within the water…all is one within love.

12 May

Within thought, words returned to me on quite a different matter 'Lead gently by the still waters of love'…'Love them into holiness'…from love, all things are possible, without a doubt now I know that this is so.

The Mountain of Delight.

1983

5 October

Since the retreat and in prayer I have been aware of light, but not clearly…peace and joy have continued and all is well. This morning I travelled into the light and experienced something I have not known before, that is, delight. There were dark mountains that had been overcome, they were not removed…but overcome…the light was the valley that lay between them. There was nothing to be seen or heard, yet it was full of the beauty of created things that had passed from this world. One dwelt on this, knowing it was for the future. Delight may seem to be a strange word – yet it is the correct word and applicable. Later this again appeared to me and I knew this delight was held in the redeemed souls of the departed, whose pain and suffering of mind, body and spirit had culminated to this 'waiting for God'. This is the light…they are the light.

6 October

I entered prayer and again was aware of the valley of delight, Travelling through this, the light intensified. There rose a mountain of solid light that shone. Its radiance reached far and wide. I attempted to climb…yet when I stopped, I had made little progress. Tiredness overcame me and I felt weary. The centre withdrew.

9 October

The mountain of light was within me…it clarified…the whole consisted of the souls of the redeemed who were ascending the mountain. It was not the mountain that was alight, the light was the myriad of souls upon it. The whole moved slowly towards the pinnacle. They stretched far back to the valley of delight. The whole was one moving and glorious light. I see the souls in this state as being very near to the Divine presence. I see it as being in conjunction with that already written some time ago, where the souls of the redeemed went within the sixth veil. There they waited, here they progress. I view with the inner eye this so beautiful and moving sight. It is called 'the mountain of longing' as those upon the ascent long for their Father…joy, rest, withdrawal.

11 October

Prayer, again the centre is shown as above, the inner 'eye' is transported to what appears to be the pinnacle. I am shown it thus within, but it is without height or depth, no beginning or end, it is a plateau upon the pinnacle, it is filled with the light that is the souls. The centre rests there for a long time. The presence of the Holy Mother is made 'known' to it. It withdraws. Much later it is again, within prayer, drawn to the plateau. There is no vision as such, it is aware of the constant movement of the souls. Again, it recollects the sixth veil. The 'known' presence of the Holy Mother here at this point is overwhelming. The realisation has just come, she was of course present within the sixth veil, and having led the souls to this point…again the centre withdraws.

12 October

Mass…later within prayer, the centre was led to the plateau. It rested here for a considerable time in contemplation…such joy and beauty is shown to the 'inner eye'. The presence of the Holy Mother was almost overwhelming in its clarity as she conducted the souls across the plateau...the plateau of devotion...the centre experiences here knowledge of total purity, total love and total acceptance, none of which is of itself but what emanates from the Holy Mother alone...it rests in adoration and withdraws.

13 October

There is such calm and peace in me. In prayer, the centre is led to the plateau. Within contemplation of this, it is 'shown' the plateau narrowing in the distance to the 'inner eye'...it watches the procession of the souls as they approach this. It is drawn to a point. As it nears, it is aware of the withdrawal of the Holy Mother's presence here...she is of the plateau only. The 'inner eye' looking forward sees a silver line, it is a path, but so narrow it is as a line. At first, it sees this as water but it is not, it is pure light. The souls proceed here accompanied by the presence of the Dove. It is drawn to contemplation of this. It recognises the narrow path as the path of wholeness. It withdraws. Thanksgiving.

16 October

Prayer and immediate awareness of all it has been recently receiving. It is drawn to the procession of souls along the narrow path of wholeness. The accompanying Dove knows each individual soul. It is very rare during these spiritual receivings that I have been aware of 'heavenly bodies' but along this path, they move with the souls. The procession is endless, the 'inner eye' is drawn forward until it is aware of further light, light that outshines all. It is 'known', rather like a solid wall. The souls pass through it, they pass through it in light, and they emerge in darkness. The light they pass through is Jesus Christ, the darkness is the beginning of the last ascent, the final ascent to the Father. This is 'known' only. The centre withdraws.

17 October

Mass and within it, the final ascent of the souls to the Father. Darkness...again awareness of 'no end'...depth, height...the pinnacle of this, the final ascent cannot be 'seen', only 'known' by faith. It is shown as an ascent, I visualise it as a mountain, but this is only that I may focus upon it. Only the base is actually 'known', but it is enough to be shown two things, one, that here on the final ascent the souls are completely alone, alone in respect that they are unaccompanied by a guide of any kind…and alone that they are not aware of any other soul…and two, is shown myriads upon myriads of paths upon the ascent, each soul 'knows' its path, it knows it by faith and it knows it by the inner eye of love. It cannot adequately be put into words the joy here…the words given within me were "In the beginning was the Word." Blessed be God.

The Mountains of Ascent

10 October 1987

For many days now within prayer has been the knowledge of a range of mountains, the base can be 'seen' but not their pinnacles which are shrouded in mist, they extend as far as the inner eye can visualise, and they are magnificent and beautiful to behold, streams of water, flowers of all kinds bloom upon them, foliage abounds, it seemed at first that no spot upon them was bare, there are however many places that are bare, but they are not easily recognised because of such luxuriant growth which masks them. It was noted, however, that the higher up the inner eye travelled, the more beautiful it became. I do not recognise this as visionary (i.e. of the eternal) but as contained within prayer in as much as it is the soul's ascent towards eternity, these are the mountains of ascent from earth to heaven which the soul attempts to ascend in its prayer life, its desire and search for the Divine. Once the ascent is begun, i.e. belief in God is recognised, it is drawn by and inspired by the Holy Spirit ever higher in its quest for spiritual fulfilment. Many of course remain at the mountains' base, for although they do believe in God, they are not sufficiently motivated to change their lives, or to allow themselves to be changed, they may wish it to be so, even long for it to be so, but earthly values are too strong and their wills are too weak to set them free. The bare patches are the times when the ascending soul is beset with fears and doubts and is as it were 'laid low' by various pressures upon it. The higher the soul does ascend, however, the less are the bare patches to be found. Far away on a distant peak, the inner eye was aware of infants and children making the ascent, I cannot explain this. I am naming these mountains that I recognise as ascending heights of prayer as the mountains of desire, and I mean the word 'desire' in this context as 'a longing for' continual and unabated prayer, especially prayer of contemplation. (It) is a longing for the fusing of the soul through Christ to the Father, to this end pray constantly through light and darkness, through whatever assails the soul – pray.

12 October

Mass yesterday morning, and within this, the inner eye saw clearly the far mountain range on which infants and children were making their ascent, it seemed to be in reverse to that of adult souls, striving through prayer to reach the summit and pass from this life. The mountains of the young were completely bare at first glance, but it was shown that as they did ascend, albeit very slowly, they left in their wake the same beauty as the adult souls strove after. These were the infant and very young souls of children that were destined by the will of God to pass from this life long before adulthood was reached, their innocent and blameless lives left behind a legacy of beauty that arose from the lessons that we are supposed to learn from them, the suffering for example of little children whose lives are cut short through disease, neglect, starvation etc, they ascend their own mountain on the prayers of others, but most of all by the compassionate prayers of angels for them. None of their lives will ever have been in vain, their mark is left forever on the earth, For each innocent soul that is gathered to the Father, somewhere a flower blooms in memory.

17 October

Prayer has been centred on the mountains of desire and this further adds to what I have written above, to constantly dwell on such beauty cannot fail to bring in its wake tranquillity, in times of darkness and dryness it sustains, as only a constant dwelling on the Trinity can do.

4 December

Mass this morning was fruitful, the inner eye was upon the mountain of desire and the soul's ascent, the higher it climbed the more beautiful it became, I do not see this as such, but recognise that the beauty that the inner eye witnesses is the reflection of the ever-ascending soul in prayer. The physical body seems to get less and less than the soul expands, until finally it is not understood as a soul within a body, rather the body within the soul. The appearance of the physical body has little meaning at this stage, although of course, it is still present, it still lives in this world but its appearance is negative, whether elderly – ugly – physical deformity etc, it is the growing beauty of the soul seeking its Maker that is of the essence. The true growth of the soul, however, will beautify the physical face, not changing its structure but showing through the expression…the eyes, the growth of divine love. It must never be forgotten by any soul that the word is ever "Watch." Watch as you were ever taught to be watchful at the very beginning of your prayer life, for the devil may arrive as a thief in the night, perhaps he covets most of all these souls nearing the end of their ascent, he would fain carry off this prize. Watch…pray…love and obey. "This commandment I give to you, that you love one another as I have loved you." These words returned to me again during this morning's Mass, perhaps they are to be my watchword!

7 December

Within prayer, the inner eye was returned to the mountain of longing…of desire…it was drawn to a soul (an unknown soul) that was nearing the shrouded pinnacle. It is not known whether this soul was old or young, in good physical and mental health or not, only that its earthly life was drawing to a close, there appeared at the edge of the shrouded pinnacle an angel clothed in purest white, the outstretched wings waited to enfold the soul as it passed over. This was shown to be the angel of death and was beautiful to behold. Death in this context was understood as welcoming and a natural end of life in this world, this soul was ready to depart and longing to continue in the life that was to be, there was no fear, for it had climbed the mountain in the full knowledge that hope would be fulfilled and truth had indeed set it free. There passed before the centre a kaleidoscope of souls in varying stages of life, upon whom the Angel of Death would descend at any given time, souls that were unprepared, who were afraid, who cling to life here at any cost, souls upon whom death would come suddenly and unexpectedly. The centre is shown that in whatever the circumstances of the soul's departure from this life, the Angel of Death never changes his demeanour, always he is light and hope, at the actual passing over, this is recognised by the soul and he is freed from earthly ties. The inner eye once again sought the soul, nearing the pinnacle but it was gone. It slowly descended the mountain until the base was visible, and devoid of any aid to prayer, i.e. it rested in darkness, it was aware that its own prayer rose upon the mountain, yet it sprung from emptiness and darkness. I understand this to mean 'pray regardless' even if it is painful, even if it is only a few words, for it will rise from the depths, rise and become part of the corporate beauty of the world's prayer. I thought back to my own recent experience of this, when 'The Lord's Prayer' was the full extent of my prayer and even this was very difficult. Yet now that I am through this, imagine the infinite beauty of this God-given prayer as it rises to the heavens, rises from pain and anguish, but flowering in eternity, this did bring home to me the importance of perseverance, we are not able to judge here the importance of continuous prayer as it is received in eternity and borne by the angels to the throne of God. This returns me in thought to what I have already written some time ago. Regarding the bridge of prayer, prayer ascends and descends. I remembered at this point Christ in Gethsemane. It was not removed from him, yet dwell upon the outcome of this, the prayer of man ascending to his Father, as the prayer of man will ever ascend to his Father until Christ comes again.

19 December

This morning, contemplation followed naturally for me, one leads to the other, although sometimes one is immediately led to contemplative prayer only. Although already written, the inner eye is not able to pierce the mist that shrouds the pinnacle of the prayer mountain, of desire, of longing, it is 'known' to the understanding without doubt, that within the mist two souls have met, the soul from this world is at the threshold, the indefinable line of earthly death, the passing over from here to eternity, it is poised for flight as it were, and hovers momentarily at the brink, it is still 'alive' to this world, yet it is fully aware of the next, to the understanding there is no regret, it is aware dimly I think of others' regret at its passing, but for this soul the time has passed where meaning in this respect is relevant any more, it has climbed its mountain, it has known the beautiful places where it has been at one with its Maker, it has known darkness and near despair, the aridity and blankness of non-prayer, it has fallen many times, yet as many times as it has fallen, it has risen, it has called and been answered, it has called and there has been no answer, although this is not strictly true, the answer has not been the expected answer, and has been given perhaps in a way that has not been recognised as an answer, it has run the gamut of human life in experiences, yet the centre is very aware that this soul is not 'old', it is realised almost as this is written that the soul is 'old' in earthly years, but young in the beauty and innocence that climbing the mountain has conferred upon it, for the higher any given soul ascends, the greater its desire for God becomes and the deeper the longing that fills it, the soul expands within and is beautiful beyond recognition. The soul's guardian angel that has dwelt within it from conception, recognised or unrecognised, now becomes a reality to him, the light that has burned consistently within, increases a hundredfold, as the soul passes over. It is his guardian that leads it…a soul's guardian angel is fully recognised by the soul in eternity and plays a very important part in the soul's journey to perfection and unity, now it is this same glorious light by which the soul is enabled to 'see' a little of the glory that is to come. By this same light it 'sees' the soul awaiting him, to receive and welcome him home. The centre withdraws.

22 December

Mass this morning and within this the return of the above, the light emanating from the soul's guardian angel intensified, and at the soul's actual passing over the gateway as it were to eternity, opened to receive it, revealing momentarily a very small part of the glory of the world to come, submitting the soul in its care with the illumination of hope fulfilled. The angelic host in the beauty befitting the messengers of God, welcome the guardian back to the realm, It is not 'known' who the soul that waits to receive the newly arrived is, neither is recognised by the centre. This is not personal to the centre at all, but representative of the whole. Suffice to say that redemption has taken place, nothing whatever of this is 'seen', it cannot be 'seen', only 'known' to the understanding. It is a very brief glimpse of something almost beyond comprehension, mysterious, yet wrapped in love's simplicity…nothing of value is without cost, but the knowledge remains, love is of the essence, hope will be fulfilled, faith will be justified. The inner eye seemed to retreat to a far place, where it stood (as it were) to gaze with delight towards the mountain of prayer.

28 December

The inner eye is drawn to the mountain of prayer, it draws the centre initially towards it, there is a grandeur about it that speaks of a living force inviting the soul to climb, strive and attain. Thoughts return of the bridge of prayer between earth and heaven, the ascending and descending prayer of the angelic host, it is also realised with considerable force how wrong it is for those on earth to seek to call back a soul that has left this world, to attempt to detain it from commencing its journey, it will do no good to any who attempt this, they stultify their own growth, that soul is within the eternal; they do return I have no doubt, but it is they who approach us here, and is always for a very specific purpose, and controlled by the guidance of the Holy Spirit. One may ponder upon the mystery, one can only write as one is guided to do, and know that truly 'without God one is nothing'.

31 December

Within prayer, the inner eye is upon the mountain of prayer/desire, almost a mystical mountain but shrouded as its pinnacle is between earth and heaven, again it is aware of the eternal soul that waits to welcome all departing souls, its light of redemption both strong and powerful, the centre is shown the necessity for this regarding all souls passing from the world to the world beyond, even a soul held in the darkness must be given hope and a glimpse of paradise if it is to be set upon the road to redemption and union, hope must never be removed, lest despair overcomes and the soul is truly lost within the darkness. The more we strive here to 'love as he loves us', the readier we shall be to undertake the journey before us, perhaps the deeper we have tried to obey Christ's command, the stronger and more revealing will be the light opening before us as we pass through this gossamer veil of 'here' to 'there', but that light is revealed to all in a certain measure, is what I have been shown, no soul is totally banished to darkness unless it rejects the love of God, if it does – then it creates its own hell.

5 January 1988

Within prayer, the inner eye was drawn again, far away from the mountain of desire...of longing, to enable the whole to be 'seen' clearly. This was dwelt upon for some time, very gradually it was aware of several other mountains, it was rather like standing on a plain in Norway, and 'seeing' at distance mountains that appeared as one range but were, in fact, separate ranges, looking very similar from afar, but being very different at closer inspection. Here, however, even at a distance, the difference was clearly recognised, there was, as far as could be understood, only one but of prayer, of desire and of longing for God. The others stood apart in their starkness, bleakness and darkness, there was an eternal iciness upon them, barren of all growth. The inner eye drew nearer to them and became aware of myriads of souls climbing towards their pinnacles, all of which were equally shrouded in the same enveloping mist that was upon the mountain of prayer. These souls were totally unaware that they were climbing towards eternity, they were living out their lives within the world, each day nearer to the end, but they lived in the darkness of unbelief, striving and seeking fulfilment found only in their desire of the spiritually dead. Their values were those of the spiritually dead, they were not yet awakened to the true reality. The centre withdrew.

7 January

Within prayer, the inner eye is returned to the mountain of darkness and upon which are countless souls, quite suddenly the whole of the mountains disintegrated and was received into the earth, taking away every soul with them. This is understood by the centre to mean that this has been brought upon them by their worldly values, their lack of vision, seeing death as they do as the end, and not the continuation of life in the world to come, death is to them the end. The centre 'looked' upon the darkness of the earth that had engulfed them, there was no sign of the light of life, as though they were already dead, but this not understood to be so, many will be saved and led to the mountain of desire, even if they remain at the base, they are there. For those that are blind and intransigent, they too receive a vision of the glory of God, remember that every soul at the moment of conception is given the guardian angel that lives within it, no matter its way of life. It is through the constant prayer of every guardian that the soul is enabled to experience this, every guardian indeed is the bearer of faith, hope and love, and strives constantly to bring the soul to God. It cannot be said that the guardian fails in its task, but that the soul is blind, its time in purgatory must of necessity be long and arduous, nobody but God knows the outcome of this. Prayer continues regardless, that finally, all shall indeed be well. The inner eye remained on the whole.

8 January

Mass, and within this, the inner eye was drawn to the souls of the 'dead', 'dead' that is to the vision and knowledge of Abba, and to their guardian angels dwelling within them. The centre pondered upon the guardians and was drawn through this, to consider its guardian and to offer for the first time thanksgiving for this gift, how lax we so often are, how much we take for granted without even an acknowledgement of the existence of love and grace bestowed upon us. The inner eye was drawn to consider the guardians at a deeper level. Are they sad, unhappy when the soul in which they live has no knowledge of the Divine, living perhaps evil and corrupt lives? Do they ever question God's purpose for them, inhabiting such a soul? No, this cannot be so, they are called by God to fulfil His purposes, they are messengers, servants of the Lord, they obey – not in blind obedience, but because they love God, and it is their privilege and joy to serve him as he wills, their prayer for the soul is constant and unremitting, and although no harvest may be reaped here, this does not mean it will never be reaped in eternity, that their essence is of 'faith, hope and love' is the crux of their ministry, this as heavenly beings, as spirit, can never fail them or be removed from them. This is God's eternal gift and in this, they live and have their being. When the day dawns when their soul is redeemed before God, how great will be their joy. The centre is returned to the base of the mountain of prayer/desire/longing and is at peace, the inner eye glances upwards towards the pinnacle fleetingly and is aware of the light.

10 January

Within prayer, the inner eye is drawn to the mountain of desire/longing and to the souls upon it, it is realised that many who perhaps are high upon it will fall from grace, even into darkness and evil, no living soul upon this earth is safe from temptation and many may subsequently fall. It is not shown, however, that they will be cast into the darkness of those souls who have never known light or accepted and acknowledged the love of God. There must surely be a residue of light left deep within their core, once the light and love of God have been received. I am not shown that it is completely eliminated. This does not detract from the seriousness of their fall from grace, but the very small light that is left gives hope of ultimate victory, they remain, however, at the foot of the mountain, perhaps until the day of their death. The centre withdraws.

12 January

The inner eye was drawn to the mountain of prayer, but from a different angle, thus giving a different perspective. People who in the world like to climb mountains do not always start from the same place, do they? Some want the easiest ascent, trying to reach the top as quickly as possible and with the least effort as possible also, some do not prepare themselves adequately and are severely injured or even killed, some deliberately choose the most difficult route, pitting their mental and physical strength against any hazard that may beset them, but those who are serious in their quest do go into it as prepared as it is possible to be, seeking advice, reading and thinking about what their intentions and hopes are before they attempt an ascent. Many prefer to go alone, others feel safer and better protected with others around them.

So, the centre was shown that the base – the starting point on the mountain of prayer has a very broad spectrum indeed, each individual soul is unique in its own individuality, even those that may well appear to be the same, are not so.

The centre was aware that this was indeed rooted within the earth and its pinnacle pierces the heavens, the bridge of prayer that the centre was shown some time ago, is not part of this mountain, the bridge is solely for the prayers of those on earth for those in heaven, especially for those for whom reconciliation is so necessary, and for the constant and continuing prayers of those already within the next world for those on earth, included here are the prayers of the angelic host for all humanity, ever descending and ascending. The mountain of prayer and desire and longing for God, with which at present the centre is concerned, is the soul's journey to God through and within its prayer life and its attempted ascent to this end. The higher it climbs, the more beautiful it becomes, and the more the mystery deepens, it is realised how very little one really knows…the inner eye rested for a long time upon this living mountain of prayer. There is, of course, one prayer that should be the beginning and end of all prayer, the complete prayer, i.e. The Lord's Prayer, the perfect prayer for all occasions, a singular and corporate prayer, a prayer to be used in the depths as well as the heights, so many books have been written on prayer for the beginner – the advanced – yet a prayer from the depths of one's being can hold all meaning and say all things as it is uttered and carried heavenwards, "Father" that in itself is a thanksgiving – an intercession, a plea, an acknowledgement of recognition, of "child", "Father", "love."

20 January

Within prayer the inner eye is upon the whole mountain of desire and longing, the knowledge that prayer rising from earth to heaven is the world's plea to its Creator for mercy, is almost overwhelming in its reality, the world pleads, the centre is halted at this point as its own prayer overtook it, its vision of the mountain deepened, everything upon it was intensified, and it became a part of the whole, an infinitesimal part, but that is what the whole consists of, every soul at prayer builds the whole, every thought and act of love is part of the whole, as is every thought and act of non-love, of violence. Again, the centre was moved back to consider the whole. This is a rather strange feeling, as though one was physically removed by an unseen force – not one's own volition – so the mountain appears far away on the skyline, yet it is known that it lives within.

21 January

Within, the centre was aware of the very gradual disappearance of the mountain of prayer from the inner eye until there was nothing, yet at the same time it knew that he inner eye was turning inwards, to rest its gaze thereupon the same mountain, for everything that is vision is from within the soul's depths, so what one has experienced perhaps for years as being beyond oneself is of oneself, one feels perhaps that one 'sees' in a context of the vision being afar off. I think this is because for a long time it cannot be understood, because one has not reached the point of being able to understand it (and maybe one never does). This does mean that one is responsible for it, if love, joy, peace are within any one vision – then this is God's work, the soul's enlightenment is from God and the more the soul is enlightened, the greater the desire for God will be. The mountain of prayer has great relevance here, for it is rooted in every soul, it is up to us whether we will seek to climb, or remain where we are. Whether it is realised or not that the vision is from within, perhaps the need to protect it from ourselves is necessary, so that we can 'see' it more clearly. If I look from a window and see a rainbow – or not – a river etc, this is not from within one, it is part of nature and recognised as such, but if I align the rainbow to the bridge of prayer between earth and heaven – the mountain as an ascent of prayer towards God – the river as the water from the side of Christ, purifying whoever enters it – then that is from within me. I have turned and used nature's gifts to literally ascend towards my Maker, this is the soul's yearning and seeking for the Divine. Once a vision has served its purpose, it must not be clung to or used as an emotional bandage for wounds that are essential for the soul's growth, one must be watchful and wary, not all visions are from God, and one should not attempt to go it alone, but seek the help of a wise spiritual director.

25 January

Within prayer, the inner eye was drawn to yet another aspect of the prayer mountain. Here again, there were many souls in various stages of growth upon it, this was dwelt upon for a long time. The mountain changed many times back and forth to the whole mountain and back to this particular part of it. There was something different about these souls but it was not yet understood.

26 January

Mass and within this, the inner eye was drawn to the mountain of prayer and desire and to the souls it was made aware of yesterday, that they were different. Suddenly it cleared, these were the souls of many different faiths and beliefs that were outside the Christian faith, yet a very real part of the family of God within the world, their prayers too rose to the Father in heaven but did not pass through the Son. I do vaguely remember writing some time ago of something similar to this that was within the eternal, and that none could come to the Father except through the Son, well, I do not know – who can know what will happen within eternity, but this prayer mountain is within ourselves in this world and every soul in this world is a child of God, to him, they pray, to him they aspire and reach out. For us as Christians, we believe the Son has come and now awaits the second coming. Through him, we seek to know the Father, for others, it is God the Father alone to whom they pray. Prayer is prayer, no matter from whom it comes, so every person that prays to God, Father, Son and Holy Spirit, or to the Father alone, is as one upon this mountain of prayer. Again, the inner eye perceived the fusing of all upon this one mountain, that we are all one in the sight of God, and again it was drawn away so that it could 'see' more clearly the beauty of the whole.

28 January

Within prayer, the inner eye was upon the mountain of prayer…desire…very slowly, it began to fall into the earth and was received within it. Where it had stood became a verdant green…a place of quiet and retreat, giving peace and tranquillity to all who came upon it, nothing had changed, it was within the soul of mankind, within every soul if they did but recognise it and act upon it.

Chapter 6 Some of Ivy Goodley's 'Visions' at Holbeach

Ivy, aged 80, in her garden in Holbeach.

Ivy's visions from July 30, 2005

30 July 2005

Silence both within and without and remained so for some time, waiting. Finally, my eyes closed and immediately the inner eye opened. The soul was alone on a shore and looking across a vast expanse of the sea towards the far horizon, the sun low in the sky. This had been received many times and always leads afresh to what it knows will be revealed. The soul longs to depart from this world and go "home." It felt itself ready and yet still remained. This was not its decision to make, this was realised, but it nevertheless still remained at a deep level. The water beckoned it, although in truth the decision was its own. Gently, it was carried forward without hindrance, drawing ever closer to that far horizon and what lay beyond. Literally, from seemingly nowhere, a small craft appeared, hands reached out and the soul was lifted from water to craft. A voice spoke softly within "not yet, not yet." The craft reached the shore, the soul once more on firm ground, the craft soon lost to sight. The soul did not move for a very long time, darkness fell, the dawn broke through and darkness fell, the dawn broke through. Finally, in broad daylight and without hesitation, the soul again entered the waters, this time it progressed much further, knowing itself to be ever closer to "home" where I so longed to be. Without warning, a violent storm lashed around it, tossing it hither and thither upon giant waves, it knew fear, it heard a voice calling out to be saved, it was some little time before it realised it was its own voice that called. Gradually the storm abated, the water calmed, fear had not left it, however, it knew not what to expect, and then again from seemingly nowhere, the same small craft appeared, hands, as before lifted it from the waters, this time there was no voice. The shore was reached, the hands lifted the soul upon it, gentle hands that seemed to speak of their own accord "Fear not, fear not" and then it was lost to sight. The soul had learnt a very hard lesson, but it had learnt and knew it must stay in this world until that voice said "Come." To use the time given, the Holy Spirit would lead it, listen and follow. Fear was removed, acceptance replaced this, thanksgiving also for what had been given. Look forward with joy…The inner eye closed, inner silence remained, but "all was indeed well." This may well apply to others, I have no way of knowing, but it was given to me I know for a reason. I do accept and I do repeat "All is well."

September 15 2005

Prayer consisted of one word, "Lord," within this one word is all prayer. After a time I was drawn to intercessory prayer, the inner eye perceived the crucifix and Our Lord upon it, there appeared to be no pain, i.e. no pain that could be recognised as physical pain and yet I knew that within him was the pain of such intensity. His eyes were open. I held each person before him, there were no longer prayers, and Our Lord knew their need. Only each name was remembered inwardly. Quite suddenly, I realised what was happening, as each one passed before him their pain was instantly absorbed within his own pain, this does not mean they were instantly relieved of it, but that he bears it with them, they are not alone. Once this truth is recognised, they are enabled to accept what they are called to bear. His love infiltrates the deepest recesses of their being and his love is the most precious of gifts they will ever receive, it strengthens where there is weakness, it deepens faith that perhaps was floundering because the soul felt so alone, even abandoned. However, many are supporting us to the best of their ability, inner loneliness weakens and even destroys, leaving in its wake despair, and despair is one of Satan's tools. Love sustains where all else may fail, this is not always easy to grasp, to understand the concept of the power of the love of Our Lord. Perhaps, many have never known the joy of human love and this may cause a hard shell to develop outwardly, a defence mechanism, perhaps many have known love but feel it is now lost to them, death, separation leaves them wounded and bereft, faith falters, weakened by grief. There may be self-blame or blaming others for what is inevitable, death is not the end but the beginning of a new life. I was silent for some time, a nothingness within and without and then that one word emerged yet again "Lord." The inner eye opens, the Cross only remains, it is empty, Love has triumphed, he rises, prayer begins and ends with that one life-giving word "Lord"…words given long ago return yet again, perhaps to emphasise what I must learn, I am learning but am not at the end of the road.

yet…

Lead gently by the still waters of love.

18 September 2005

I thought, as I have often done before, that it was complete, apparently not. Prayer began as before with the one word "Lord" nothing else, no further words, again, after a considerable time, the crucified Lord was before the inner eye, souls passing endlessly before him. I noted finally one such was kneeling in an attitude of silent prayer and every passing soul made a slight detour around it, not before it, but round it. There was no recognition from them who it might be. For one fleeting moment, I assumed it was myself, intercessory prayer, but quickly realised I was alive and within this world. The inner eye focused upon this one unknown soul looking for a sign of recognition, this too seemed timeless, no concept of time at all. The eyes of the Lord fully open, although, obviously aware of the endless flow passing before him, nevertheless, never wavered from this one soul in obeisance before him. Finally, it was as though a brilliant light illuminated the crucified Lord and this one soul. This soul, moved and was immediately one within the passing souls. The Lord's eyes closed, the inner eye followed the Light surrounding the soul as it moved away very gradually and so slowly I did not at first realise what was happening, it separated itself from the others, the inner eye could see the Light only and follow. This alternated between darkness and light – night and day until its final destination was reached. I was not prepared for what I was shown, silence within and without, but acknowledgement then, it was Mary, the greatest intercessor of all, had returned to the place of his birth from the place of his death. "Holy Mary, Mother of God, pray for us sinners now and at the hour of our death Amen."

20 September 2005

Yet again, a continuation of what I considered as final. The holy Mother looked within the manger where her infant son had lain, it was of course empty, but within her being she was aware of him as clearly as though he slept before her. She looked at his hands and his feet, flawless as the newly born are, his head and fine crown of hair upon it. At the same moment came immediately to her the man upon the cross, the infant he had been as one with the man he had become. A mother must allow her child freedom to be himself, not as she, with the truest of intentions, wishes him to be, he must travel his own road. Our Lord's mother heard him say from his mouth this fact "Who are my mother and my brothers?" This is in Matthew, Mark and Luke. Allow your child to go and you remain forever in his heart, cling to him and he may be lost to you. Even if all appears well on the surface, this does not mean it is so, for within him resentment may build and foster to the detriment of both. "Let go, let God" is an excellent maxim (Simone Weil). Not easy, but who said it would be easy? The inner eye returned to the Holy Mother, once more light enveloped her and all was gradually withdrawn. John 19 and Jesus's words from the cross "Dear woman," as he gave her to the care of John.

14 November 2005

Prayer, one word "Lord" inwardly intercessory prayer, each person/situation passing silently before the crucifix. Later, a nothingness, not emptiness within, rather a dwelling upon that was not centred on objects, a blankness that the inner eye was unable to pierce. Perhaps it could be described as a division between the worlds we live in on the one hand as opposed to a knowledge of something beyond that could neither be seen nor ever fully understood and yet a surety that it was present. Although this blankness/division was a reality, nevertheless, it was perceived that very minute pinpoints of Light infiltrated here and there. The inner eye dwelt upon this for a long time, they neither increased nor decreased and even with the keenest of sight it was 'known' to be impossible to see through them as humanity would understand the perception of anything beyond. A reassurance was, however, received that although hidden, does not mean non-existence. The word 'reassurance' has been used and it may be queried how the writer was reassured. Thus can only be explained as a movement of the Holy Spirit within the depths who is known to be present. There may seem to be emptiness around, but never within the soul wherein he dwells recognised or unrecognised, the Holy Spirit 'is'. The inner eye rested for a long time upon these pinpoints of Light. Finally, the eye closed, reopening almost immediately to what appeared to be a blank wall that could not and was not meant to be penetrated. Nevertheless, what has been received remains to reinforce Faith, Hope and that most important word Love within which lives the "All" – There followed silently the prayer of thanksgiving.

19 November (written out on 25 November) 2005

There came within a knowledge of water, pure and crystal clear, the inner eye dwelt upon this for some time until it was realised they were the waters of love, they flowed slowly towards the wall of blankness, this 'wall' was not to be confused with a solid brick wall, rather, as formerly described, a blankness. As the waters slowly moved forward, the minute pinpoints of Light enlarged and the larger they became, the more brilliantly they shone. They finally moved closer and closer together until they became one Light, at this point, they descended into the slowly moving waters and were within them. The waters flowed faster towards the blankness and all around was inextinguishable Light, the waters slowed and finally were still… the Darkness is difficult to describe, it can only be said there appeared to be no point where it could be pierced, unyielding, I was reminded of a battlefield, the armies advancing towards each other, even as these thoughts surfaced the inner eye was aware of a sudden movement from the waters, sudden and overwhelming in their strength, they rose up and moved forward at tremendous speed shattering and destroying darkness, all disintegrated before their power. Once more, the representation of evil was destroyed, Light enclosed within Love was victorious.

26 November 2005

This morning, I knew I was going to have to make a promise to God and I was going to find this very difficult, once made I could not possibly break it, I made various excuses to myself as to why I should do this knowing at the same time that I had to, finally, I did so, this, to my amazement and joy was followed immediately by Spiritual Communion, so unexpectedly given, all is indeed well, now, I continue along my given path. I am not disclosing here – or to any person – what I have promised, God knows…'Thanks be to thee'.

2 May 2006

The darkness has remained, sometimes it appears to intensify to such a degree that I am almost overwhelmed and become low almost to depression, but I do recognise it for what it is and eventually, it lifts. Earlier today, this happened and immediately the crucified figure of Our Lord appeared within, it disappeared equally swiftly but it had been given. After a silent period which I used for intercessory prayer, drawn, as it had been previously into the darkness, the crucifix reappeared, at its foot lay the infant Jesus, no sound, no cry. He lay still, but his eyes gazed upwards toward the face of Christ the man. The infant left the manger rising slowly upward until he reached the heart of the man and was swiftly drawn within this still-beating heart and 'seen' no more. The manger was gone, darkness slowly enclosed the whole. I dwelt upon this, I am shown no reason, no explanation of 'why?' I leave it and wait. Later, the beating heart of the infant is the beating heart of the man – they are one. This applies to us all, we eventually become adults with all the faults of character, but also with the good within that will hopefully be stronger to combat evil. So much goes to form a child's character…This does not apply to our Lord as either infant or man, for he is God. Once more darkness envelops the whole…intercessory prayer followed.

5 May 2006

Early morning, I was wide-awake, too early to take the first medication of the day. I lay still. A shaft of brilliant Light came, within this light, the Cross could be 'seen', not the crucifix, the Cross, the Light was withdrawn leaving the Cross, this too was briefly held before being withdrawn leaving behind the darkness, rather that of the dawn breaking through, daylight, inwardly I was made aware of my path i.e. the path I am called to proceed along until life ends in this world. I experienced a sensation of freedom, no doubt I shall fall again but will be enabled to rise and continue my journey in the sure and certain knowledge of the presence of the Holy Spirit within. The shaft of brilliant Light returned briefly and awareness of it illuminated the path of Silence. Prayer of thanksgiving. Once more, I believe this to be vaguely repetitive of that received some time ago, if so, then it serves to reinforce what I already believe and is given for a specific reason applying to the inner life. I do not question it, nor ask "Why?"…accept what is received and leave it there.

As I have written before, my last silent words before I go to sleep are "Into thy hands I commend my spirit." Last night, as this happened there came inwardly a Light that flooded the path I was upon and on which I had to travel until my life ends, aware I was being led ever forward, the darkness appears to have been withdrawn although one can never be sure it will not at some point return, one day at a time! But now I am guided by this Light and when, not if I fall, it enables me to rise again and continue my way, I realise I must not allow complacency to enter…This is about the third time this brilliant Light has illuminated not only my path, but my gradual understanding and acceptance, again, perhaps to verify and strengthen my resolve(Thanksgiving) to persevere and reinforce, human frailty rather reminds me of a newly built brick wall where a few bricks are out of line, thus weakening the whole.

21 October 2008

The day begins with good intentions – these quickly fade away as reality overtakes me. One thing after another overwhelms my good intentions. I am aware within of a sense of failure. I tend to give in under pressure. I promised myself that I would not 'give in'. The promise is broken, I am weak. I say inwardly 'not my fault, it is because I am old'. I am silent, within the silence I 'hear' a voice from far away. "Where is your faith?" An ever-present assurance that 'All shall be well'. "Come, be strong, the Lord is with you."

Hold fast – All indeed 'shall be well'.

A heavyweight is lifted from me. I say inwardly, "Thanks be to thee, O Lord."

This is the last entry in Ivy's spiritual diary. She has angina and other illnesses and is increasingly in need of care. Eventually, she is transferred to a nursing home in Spalding where she remains until her death on 17 July 2012.

The question remains "What is the promise made on 26 November 2005, which she has found it so hard to keep?" In the context of her visionary experience a little earlier than this and my own experience visiting her in Holbeach and in Spalding, the promise which she found so hard to keep was the promise not to question God why she was still alive when she wanted so much to die and be with him. It came up regularly in our conversation and usually in the context of the crucifix hanging in her room. She just wanted to depart and be with Christ but her life continued much longer than she wished because of her medication.

An Epilogue

A poem was written by Ivy on 30 December 1993

So long a journeying, darkness to light,
Endless winding paths through thorn and briar.
Fair fields…sun and shadow…perfumed flowers.
Each day questioning, "Is this the final curtain?"
Comes a new dawn stealthily approaching,
On and on I walked…I ran…laughing and crying,
Slowly…slowly now.
Youth, lost in the mists of time, smiles with
Whimsy,
Neither longing for days that are as dust
Or nights of sweetest memories,
No more…no more.
Petals fall.
"So fall," I say.
The final bloom is yet to be
Not here…not here,
But in eternity.
Ivy.